THE PURPLE GANG

ORGANIZED CRIME IN DETROIT

1910-1945

Paul R. Kavieff

BARRICADE BOOKS • NEW JERSEY

Published by Barricade Books Inc.
185 Bridge Plaza North
Suite 308-A
Fort Lee, NJ 07024
www.barricadebooks.com
New Introduction © 2005 by Paul R. Kavieff
Copyright © 2000 by Paul R. Kavieff
All Rights Reserved.

The Library of Congress has catalogued the hardcover edition as
follows:

Library of Congress Cataloging-in-Publication Data

Kavieff, Paul R.
    The Purple Gang : organized crime in Detroit, 1910-1945 / Paul
R. Kavieff
        p. cm.
        1. Gangs--Michigan--Detroit--History--20th century. 2.
Organized crime--Michigan--Detroit--History--20th century. 3.
Purple Gang (Organized Crime Group : Detroit, Mich.) I. Purple
Gang (Organized Crime Group : Detroit, Mich.) II. Title

HV6439.U7 D475 2000
364.1'06'6077434--dc21
ISBN 1-56980-147-9 (hc)
ISBN 1-56980-281-5 (pb)
                                                    00-028903
First Printing
Printed in Canada

Contents

Dedication

I would like to dedicate this book to my wife,
Deborah A. Carson.

Acknowledgments

This book would not have become a reality without the help and support of many people. I would like to thank Pat Zacharias and her staff at the Detroit News Reference Library for their valuable help over a period of years; Thomas Featherstone of the Reuther Library, Wayne State University; Dave Poremba of the Burton Historical Collection, Detroit Public Library; Sharon Brown of the Michigan State Police, Central Records Division; John Currie and Mary Zumeth of the Michigan State Archives; the late Max Silk, who spent many hours with me sharing his memories about the Prohibition era; Penelope A. Morris, owner of the P. A. Morris Co., for her help in editing and creating a hard copy of the work; Stephen Rosman; Heidi Christein; Pat Henahan; Richard J. Smith and his family; my colleagues and friends in the Engineering Unit at Wayne State University; Dave Rosen; Harry "Harry the Hat" Stone, a former Purple; Richard Bak; Patterson Smith; Mike Webb; Bill Helmer; and Loren D. Estleman. A special thanks to my editor, Allan J. Wilson, for his valuable advice, and to the publishers, Carole and Lyle Stuart, for making the Purple Gang story a reality.

Preface

The Purple Gang: Organized Crime in Detroit 1910-1945 was first published in June of 2000. It was the first written history of one of the most notorious organized crime groups in the twentieth century. The original hardcover edition sold through several printings—witnessing unprecedented success for what was considered a "regional" title.

It gives me great pleasure to have the opportunity to introduce the paperback edition of The Purple Gang. Since the book's release in 2000, I have attended more than 100 book signings and have delivered lectures about Prohibition in Southeast Michigan to a wide variety of audiences. During that time I had the opportunity to meet some of the relatives of Purple Gang members, as well as other people who had grown up during the Prohibition era and knew some of the Purple Gangsters. One of the things that I actually found most interesting about the relatives of the Purples that I met was how little they actually knew about the workings of the gang or about their kinship ties. Obviously, the discussion of a gangster relative was not a topic at the dinner table. Nevertheless, some people shared some very interesting anecdotal stories about their experiences with various members of the gang.

A brother of a Purple gangster relayed an interesting story to me one evening when I asked him if he knew Harry Fleisher. Fleisher was a significant Purple who actually grew up with key members of the gang. One night in the Fall of 1935, Fleisher appeared at the door of the restaurant on 12th Street which was owned by this man's family. It was near closing time, and Fleisher asked the young teenager if he could close the restaurant early and help him count some money. "We weren't very busy so I agreed," said the man. "I spent more than three hours helping Harry count out the $125,000 he was carrying in his overcoat. When we got through, Harry tossed me a five-dollar bill for my help. After that I always considered him cheap." Whether the money represented the proceeds of a bank robbery, extortion, or one of the many money-making rackets in which Fleisher had a hand, nobody will ever know.

Another man told me that when he was drafted into the Army during World War II, a Purple Gangster named Hymie Cooper was among the inductees shipped out with him. "Cooper bullied me in boot camp, constantly shoving and playing practical jokes. Finally I wrote a letter to my father, who was a business acquaintance of Joey Bernstein, one of the bosses of the Purple Gang. My father went to see Bernstein, then he sent me a letter with a note in it addressed to Cooper from Bernstein. All the note said was, 'if anything happens to this kid, don't come back to Detroit.' That was the end of my problem," explained the gentleman. "From that time on, Cooper was as friendly as he could possibly be. In fact he followed me everywhere offering his help. I couldn't get rid of him."

The Purple Gang essentially self-destructed in the early thirties, yet their legacy lives on today. It is a story of some of the worst excesses in the environment spawned by the Eighteenth Amendment and National Prohibition. It is also the story of greed and how official corruption once reached to the pinnacle of local law enforcement and city government in Detroit. It was this corruption that allowed the Purples to flourish during the era that bankrolled what we know today as organized crime. It was also in the end that same vicious greed that brought down the Purple Gang. I truly hope you enjoy this book.

—Paul R. Kavieff
Royal Oak Michigan
February 2005

Chapter *1*

Origins of the Purple Gang

"These boys are not like other boys of their age, they're tainted, off color."

"Yes," replied the other shopkeeper. "The whole bunch of them are Purple, they're a Purple Gang."

—Hastings Street Shopkeepers,
circa 1918

It all began in 1902 when a young shoemaker named Harry Bernstein arrived in Detroit with his wife and children. The family established a small shoe repair shop located at 401 Gratiot Avenue on the city's Lower East Side, not far from Detroit's Jewish ghetto district.

Making a living was a challenging task for immigrants in those years. Bernstein, a Polish Jew, moved with his family from Russia to the tenement section of Manhattan's Lower East Side. The first years in America were the most difficult, one had to learn a new language and adapt to a new culture.

Bernstein's eldest son Abe was the second of seven children. Young Abe spent his childhood years growing up fast on the streets of New York City.

After scratching out a living in New York, Harry finally saved enough money to open a small shop of his own. The competition in New York City was tough. The country-like atmosphere of turn of the century Detroit was more welcoming, and so became the site of Bernstein's first shop.

When the Bernstein family moved to Detroit the city was on the verge of an enormous population and industrial explosion which brought on disease, overcrowded housing, poverty and an increase in crime.

The elder Bernstein and his wife spent long hours in their small shop struggling to support their growing family. During their first years in Detroit they lived in a small apartment above their shop. A second son, Joseph, came after Abe, followed by Jennie, Raymond, Ida, and Isadore.

Although Bernstein's eldest son Abe was a bright child with obvious potential, he didn't show interest in school. He was a streetwise 9-year-old by the time the family moved to Detroit. He dropped out to hawk newspapers in the business district, and then worked for Ford Motor Company to help support the family.

By the time Abe married he'd started working in the thriving Detroit area gambling houses. Gambling, technically illegal, had developed into a racket nourished by payoffs to politicians and police officials.

He became a skilled card dealer and stickman. He also met the most important politicians, police officials, and underworld figures of the era.

Abe's younger brothers Joe, Raymond, and Isadore (Izzy) fended for themselves on the streets. Theirs was a Jewish ghetto that stretched from Jefferson Avenue to East Grand Boulevard. Its outer boundaries extended a little more than two blocks east and west of Hastings Street.

Many future Purple gangsters came from this neighborhood. Their parents were for the most part working class, non-Orthodox Jews. Hastings Street, known as "Paradise Valley," was bustling with activity during the teens and early twenties. It was a heavily industrialized area where children played on soot-covered streets

Hucksters peddled their wares from pushcarts and replenished them at the nearby Eastern Market. Saloons and disorderly houses catered to the needs of factory workers at all hours of the day or night as shifts let out at the manufacturing plants.

The children of these immigrants saw their parents work long hours, yet earn only enough to provide bare necessities. They also saw men who seemed to live the good life without working.

These other men drove luxury sedans, wore the best clothes and carried thick wads in their pockets. Most of their day was spent lounging around pool halls, gambling joints, and neighborhood saloons. They were accorded a disproportionate amount of courtesy by local policemen, who ignored cars parked in front of fire hydrants or even on the sidewalk. They were gangsters.

Gangsters gambled on everything from crap games to race horses. They even made large wagers on the sandlot baseball and football games between neighborhood children.

Joe Bernstein was destined to become one of these men. Known as "Little Joey" because of his small physical stature, he developed a reputation as a "shtarker"—

a Yiddish term meaning tough guy. His younger brothers Ray and Izzy could hold their own in any brawl but Joey was the roughest of them all.

By adolescence the Bernstein Brothers were beyond their parents' control. They were sent to the Bishop ungraded school. The Old Bishop School was divided into two sections: regular students and problem children, for whom the ungraded section was a trade school. It was there that the Bernstein Brothers met other tough kids from the neighborhood.

Among them were: Harry, Louis, and Sam Fleisher; Philip and Harry Keywell; Morris Raider; Harry Altman; and Abe Zussman. There was also Sam Bernstein; Sam and Ben Purple; Zigmund Selbin; Irving Shapiro; Jack Budd; and Sam Davis. All would gain notoriety as gangsters. So much for reform school.

Although there was several years age difference among the boys, this group formed the nucleus of a local juvenile street gang which quickly became a nuisance to the peddlers, shopkeepers, and residents.

Classes at the Old Bishop School served as the gang's daily rendezvous. The boys stayed after classes on the infrequent days they attended to hang around crap games in the schoolyard that were organized by local underworld figures. It was during this period that the "Boys," as the Purples would later refer to themselves, became acquainted with the neighborhood racketeers and gamblers. "Trombeniks," the boys' parents called these underworld characters, a Yiddish term meaning a bum or a no-good person, and warned their children to stay away.

The older mobsters had a strong influence on the boys. The young Purples would run errands for them.

As they grew older and more experienced they ran schoolyard crap games and went on jobs for the older thugs, often paid a few dollars for committing crimes that could put them in prison for years.

For several years before and during the First World War, the juvenile Purple Gang terrorized the old Detroit Jewish quarter. They stole from shops and ganged up on other children. As they grew older they became bolder, rolling drunks and extorting protection money from local businessmen, even looting boxcars in the local freight yards and battling other juvenile gangs.

It was an environment not unlike the slums of Manhattan's Lower East Side, Chicago's infamous "Levee" District, or the depressed and congested areas of any large city of the era. Gangs of youths of every ethnic background fought and sometimes killed each other over imaginary slights, perceived territory, or just plain boredom.

It is important to recognize that these youngsters made a choice. Although from poverty, the majority were provided with food and shelter. The juvenile Purples were largely made up of children of recently immigrated Eastern European Jews, law abiding and hard-working families fleeing centuries of religious and cultural persecution in Europe. The older people were content to work hard and to build something for themselves and their children.

But these youngsters perceived the American dream of freedom and economic success differently than their parents. Their behavior was a product of the streets. Their idea of a rich gangster lifestyle coupled with illegal opportunities provided by Prohibition, paved the way for the bloody ascent of the Purple Gang to the top of Detroit's underworld.

Exactly how the name evolved has been open to dispute. The moniker did not come into popular use by the media until 1927. Even during its heyday in the late twenties, members openly denied the existence of any underworld organization called the Purple Gang.

In a newspaper interview with Purple gangsters who had been jailed for violating Prohibition laws in 1929, all unanimously denied the existence of the Gang. Purple gangster Joe "Honey" Miller told the press, "This Purple Gang stuff makes me sick . . . all the time the Purple Gang! Who got up that name? Everybody's a Purple. I talk to a guy a minute—the police spot him as a Purple. I have friends—they're Purples."

In the same interview, Isadore Bernstein added, "What am I in here for? How should I know? The coppers throw me in the can every now and then on general principle. They hear . . . so much they believe it themselves."

Although the name's origins are unknown, there are several theories. One credits two shopkeepers in the old Hastings Street district with its invention. One man supposedly said, "Those boys are tainted, off color."

"Purple, that's what they are," replied the other. "The whole bunch of them, they're all Purple."

In reality the name was probably the invention of a journalist, as were the shopkeepers' remarks. Whatever its origins, "Purple Gang" stuck from the late twenties on, climaxing with the gang's meteoric rise to power. It equalled terror for people on both sides of the law.

Organized crime was relatively new to America. In order to deal with its complicated gangs, it became common for police to take a "show up photo" when a group of suspects were arrested. Some of those group mug shots might contain as many as 15 or 20 suspects. Once the photographic print was completed each person would be given a rogues gallery identification number. The rogues gallery number used in group photos and individual mug shots was then cross-referenced with arrest records, biographical information, and confidential reports.

If police suspected that more than one person was involved in a crime, any members of the original group photo could be arrested and questioned. Unfortunately, less dangerous people arrested in a pool hall or blind pig raid ended up in "show up" photos with seasoned mobsters. A guilt-by-association mentality developed in the Detroit Police Department and a suspect with no gang affiliation could be labeled a Purple Gangster.

At that time, police questioning consisted of "shellacking," "massaging," or "breaking the news." It was not unusual for a suspect to receive a severe beating at the hands of the police. A writer of the period claimed that in 70 percent of cases solved, physical force had been used to elicit a confession.

Methods of interrogation varied according to the inquisitor, the police station, and who a suspect was. Someone politically connected would not suffer the same fate as someone who was not. The attitude was best summed up in the words of an early twenties desk sergeant to a rookie patrolman:

> "They may beat you in court, the complainant may not show up, they may jump their bail, politicians may interfere, there are several ways they can beat you but this, (pointing to the bruises on the suspect) they've got and make no mistake about it. There's more religion in the end of a nightstick than in any sermon, preached to the likes of them."

Another procedure made necessary by organized crime was the "Police Loop," or "the Loop." A suspect would be registered under one of their aliases, which were sometimes quite extensive, and sent from one precinct to another ("running the loop"). This kept their lawyer and bondsman from locating them in order to obtain a hearing and bail.

Legal counsel called the system unconstitutional, but police claimed it was not meant to deprive suspects of their rights, rather to let officers familiarize themselves with different suspects for identification on the streets. The real reason, of course, was to alienate gangsters from their lawyers.

Police favored the system because really serious charges would prompt the suspect to jump bail. The loop could hold a suspect long enough to gather evidence. It was also an effective form of harassment to induce an underworld figure to leave the city.

The Reign Begins

On May 1st, 1918, a significant event took place in Michigan. The State Prohibition Referendum approved in 1916 became law. Detroit was the first major American city to go completely dry as an experiment to test the dry law for the rest of the country.

The Eighteenth Amendment would prove one of the biggest errors in legislative judgment America ever made. Newfound wealth from the manufacture, importation and sale of illegal liquor helped finance organized crime in America.

Prohibition spawned rackets to provide people with alchohol and corrupted every level of Government. It provided the means for mobsters to own legitimate businesses and allowed organized crime to weave its presence irreparably into the fabric of American social and political life.

The Purple Gang graduated from juvenile delin- quents to mobsters with the rackets that new liquor laws inspired. An influx of gangsters looking to exploit Prohibition became affiliated with the Purples. Their willingness to do the Purples' dirty work extended the gang's reach, guaranteeing their dominance.

It was during this time that the still juvenile gang introduced the underworld expression "making their bones" in reference to committing murders, creating reputations for ferocity with harsh beatings, and creat- ing contacts within other mobs.

By now Abe Bernstein was removed from street level and consulted by younger Purples. He and a small group of men lead various Purple Gang factions. This group included: Charles Leiter; Henry Shorr; Raymond and Joe Bernstein; Sam Solomon; Mike Gelfand; Charles Auerbach and Jack Selbin.

The MO's

Jack Selbin, one of the first illegal merchants, sold liquor from the back of a fake storefront. He was rumored to have placed his infant son in a high chair in its front window. The sight of a patrolman's uniform caused the baby to start crying, warning Selbin and his associates to put it under wraps.

❖❖❖

Charles Auerbach was considered one of the elder statesmen of the Detroit Jewish mobs. Known as the "Professor" because of his polished appearance and refinement, he was a self-taught man who collected rare books. Like Abe Bernstein, he operated from behind the scenes.

Auerbach had come from New York City, pimping and acting as a strike breaker on Manhattan's Lower East Side. He was suspected to have been behind most of the the Purple Gang crimes during the prohibition era, his funeral was attended by some of the most important members of the Detroit underworld.

He was the first gangster of notoriety to be convicted under the Public Enemy Law in 1931. When sentenced to a fine or ninety days in jail, he calmly peeled a $100 bill from his roll and walked.

❖❖❖

Mike Gelfand was known as "One-Armed Mike" for his missing limb. One of the leaders of the Little Jewish Navy, Mike was a combination blind pig operator/racketeer. In later years Gelfand would own the "Famous Graceland Ballroom."

❖❖❖

Sam Solomon was one of the biggest bookmakers in Detroit and the brains behind the "Little Jewish Navy" faction of the Purple Gang. He was also rumored to be silent partners in his bookmaking operation with future Superintendent of Police Fred Frahm.

❖❖❖

Raymond Bernstein started out in the Detroit gambling rackets running errands. He worked as a card dealer, hijacker, strong arm man, and gunman until starting his blind pig, the "Kibbutzer Club." Ray was a smooth talking and intelligent man prone to diplomacy, but not opposed to violence when necessary. He was also a fastidious dresser and ladies' man.

❖❖❖

Joe Bernstein came out of the Oakland Sugar House Gang, which spawned the Purple Gang. He was reputed to be the toughest of the four Bernstein brothers and a dangerous man to cross. His criminal career built a bankroll upon which he eventually financed a legitimate oil business and ditched the Purples for the life of a prosperous businessman.

❖❖❖

Henry Shorr and Charles Leiter had been members of the Oakland Sugar House Gang, the mentors of the Purples (many Purples were former Sugar House thugs). Well-known in the Detroit underworld for their ability to design and build efficient liquor-producing plants, their distillery was one of the finest ever seized. It was reputed to be worth $125,000.

❖❖❖

Beating Prohibition

The home-brewing of wine and beer for personal consumption was legal under the provisions of the Volstead Act. Sugar outlets, or "sugar houses," were principal suppliers of the products needed to make home brew. It was legal to sell products to make alcohol for home consumption only. Many legitimate suppliers catered to underworld brewers who in turn mass-produced for "blind pigs," establishments where liquor was sold illegally.

Michigan was declared officially dry by 1918. There were 1,534 licensed saloons and 800 unlicensed blind pigs in Detroit. By 1925 the number of blind pigs was estimated between 15,000 and 25,000.

Chapter *2*

The Birth of the Oakland Sugar House Gang

"All of us started carrying guns back in 1923 in the old Sugar House Days. One of our Jewish boys killed a Dago named Speed on Hastings Street. Then all hell broke loose."

—Izzy Schwartz, Sugar House Gangster

The Purple Gang rose to power in the mid-twenties as a result of two occurrences. The first was when the newly formed Purples aligned themselves with the older Oakland Sugar House Gang. They saw the old-timers as a tool for becoming a respected gang.

The second occurred in 1923, while Sugar House gangster and proprietor Isadore Cantor, strolled down Hendrie Street on Detroit's East Side. As he turned the corner he noticed a touring car pull to the curb ahead of him. The driver climbed out and they casually made eye contact.

In that split second of recognition both men reached for their hip pockets and gunfire echoed in the street. The touring car driver staggered several steps before crumpling to the ground. Women screamed and people scrambled for cover while Cantor shoved the smoking pistol in his pocket and disappeared into the forming crowd.

Later Cantor walked into the Bethune Street Police Station and turned himself in for murder. He'd shot Frank Speed, an associate of a gang shaking down local bootleggers and independent blind pig operators. The gunman had languished in the hospital for several hours and then died.

Frank Speed came to Detroit from New York City with a lengthy police record. He fled the city following a hold-up but was returned and convicted of armed robbery. Sentenced to seven years in the state prison of Southern Michigan, he was paroled after serving two and a half.

During the inquiry into the Speed shooting, Cantor told police that he and his partner George Goldberg operated a wholesale sugar business. The "Sugar House," as the operation was called, was a legitimate business which dealt in brewing products. Its purpose was to cater to those who wanted to home-brew.

A prescribed amount of beer and wine could be made under the Prohibition law for personal consumption. The boom in corn sugar production during Prohibition was one of the most spectacular agricultural events of the twenties. Corn sugar was a popular brewing ingredient because it leaves no ash and no odor—ideal for large scale underworld brewing.

During the early twenties, Speed's mob had an interest in a greyhound racetrack. One of the ways the gang made money on it was by forcing underworld operators to buy hundreds of dollars worth of betting slips. If the "offer" was rejected, the victim would be intimidated until he folded under the pressure of their extortion.

One fateful day in 1923, Frank Speed showed up at Isadore Cantor's Sugar House and offered to sell him $250 worth of dog track slips. Cantor, well aware of what was happening, politely refused. Speed knew the Oakland Sugar House was lucrative and pushed the issue, threatening to tell Prohibition authorities.

Cantor still refused and Speed stormed out of the Sugar House, mumbling threats.

Cantor then received anonymous threatening letters and phone calls almost daily. Both men were under severe stress, and neither knew they would see the other on the street that day. By then they'd become so highly strung that their trigger fingers had minds of their own.

Cantor was actually exonerated in the killing of Speed, based on a ruling of justifiable homicide. It was typical of the luck of the Sugar House Gang. Its survival despite its gangsters' impossible odds of being jailed or killed would carry into the Purple Gang's life span, a fortuity due as much to bullying cops and other criminals as it was to blind luck.

Cantor may have killed Speed out of self preservation, but he was still a target of revenge for the dead man's gang. Two months later, while Cantor stood in front of a restaurant with friends, a maroon sedan seen earlier pulled slowly up to the curb.

For a brief, silent moment passersby stared at the silhouettes inside the vehicle. Suddenly the air was filled with bullets and debris. Police would later estimate that 50 to 100 rounds of ammunition had been fired at the group, right in broad daylight.

A Cantor bodyguard was the first to go down in the attack. The attacker had fired indiscriminately into the crowd. Threats by Speed's gang in retaliation for his killing had finally become a reality, yet Cantor was still alive.

He identified the gunmen from the hospital but was offered $5000 not to testify with the stipulation that he leave Detroit permanently. Cantor failed to appear at trial. The charges were dismissed without prejudice.

According to Detroit Police the only reason Cantor had been offered hush money was because Speed's gang found it impossible to eliminate him. Cantor's absence at trial was soon to be explained to police. In early April of 1924, his bullet-riddled body was fished out of the East River in New York City. No one was arrested in connection with the murder.

All of the killings and turmoil had really been the result of the power struggle between the gang in control of the Sugar House operation—the Sugar House Gang—and the gangs that wanted to conquer them. Despite their murder of Isador Cantor, Speed's gang never gained control of the Oakland Sugar House.

Evidence suggests that Purples' Henry Shorr and Charles Leiter were active in the Oakland Sugar House business since its inception. It was Leiter and Shorr who continued to operate the house after Cantor's death.

When the house first opened, Isadore Cantor et al had been front men for Charles Leiter, Henry Shorr, and other mobsters who made the business prosper by selling supplies to underworld brewers as well as operating their own plants. It was Leiter and Shorr who kept Cantor alive for so long after the Frank Speed shooting, making him impossible to hit.

Shorr and Leiter surrounded themselves with tough young men who would become the Purple Gang. They were expert at the installation and concealment of high capacity brewing plants with excellent product. These operations were funded with money from hijacking and extortion rackets.

The Oakland Sugar House would become the financial bulwark of the Purple Gang because of Henry Shorr's business acumen. The gang became so powerful that they controlled prices of bootleg liquor in Detroit, financed moonshiners, and ran their own blind pigs. They dwarfed their competition when they developed nationwide underworld alliances with the New York and Chicago mobs.

According to one investigator, "The Sugar House Gang became a gang within a gang allied by birth, friendships, and by illegitimate enterprise." A number of their gunmen came from New York, imported by Shorr and Leiter as muscle. The core group of Detroit Purples included: Harry Fleisher aka "H.F."; Hyman Altman aka "the Indian"; Jacob Silverstein aka "Scotty"; Sam Davis aka "the Gorilla"; Isadore Kaminsky aka "Uncle"; Abe Zussman aka "Abie the Agent"; Sam Bernstein aka "Fatty"; Joe Miller aka "Honey"; Lou Fleisher; Jack Budd; Raymond and Joe Bernstein; Lou Gellerman; Jacob Levites; Ben Marcus; and John Wolff.

Most of these men were eight to twelve years younger than Leiter or Shorr and would form the nucleus of the "Purple Gang."

The Soldiers of the Purple Gang

Harry Fleisher or H.F., in the idiom of the underworld, started his criminal career as a truck driver and bodyguard for Charlie Leiter. In his capacity as Oakland Sugar House driver, Fleisher would fill corn sugar and brewing supply orders. The address would be near the site of someone else's hidden still or cache of completed product.

If he found it, he would return with several others and either steal or hijack the load of liquor, depending on whether the location was guarded. One of his favorite tricks was to locate the storage area and kick in the door. He'd locate a bum loafing nearby and offer the man a few dollars to load the truck.

When the man came around to the cab to collect his money, he would get the muzzle of Fleisher's gun instead. The loaded truck would pull away, leaving the body of the laborer where it fell. From these exploits, Harry Fleisher became known and feared in the underworld as a man who did his own work.

If a competing mobster encroached on one of his rackets, he would give the man a polite warning to back off. His second warning was a meal with the man who, when finished eating, would be shot in the head.

Sam Davis was known as "the Gorilla" because of his simian appearance and low I.Q. He was used to ferret out hidden cases of bootleg liquor at a still site. He also provided other gangsters with entertainment when describing its location. Davis liked to use the word partition to describe a wall and would mispronounce it "pishmission."

His excitement grew with his description. Hardened gangsters would double over with glee at the sound of

Davis repeatedly talking about liquor behind the pish-mission. But Davis was also an experienced strong arm man or "shtarker" who would not hesitate to use a gun or knife on an unwary enemy. Although unsophisticated for use in sensitive jobs, he was a very effective muscleman and collector.

Hyman Altman, aka "Two Gun Harry" and "the Indian" because of his resemblance to a Native American, started out running errands for the Sugar House Mob and was referred to as the office boy of the Purple Gang. At 5'8" and 200 pounds he was a fearsome-looking thug who, ironically, was not very tough.

Because of his formidable stature, the Russian born Altman was effective at strong arm work as long as he carried a gun or a knife.

Jacob Silverstein was a schoolmate of the original group of Purples in the old Hastings Street neighborhood. Apparently the only one who paid attention in class, he would eventually gain fame as bookkeeper for the Purple Gang.

Jack Budd was another strong arm man. Also born in Russia and brought to America as an infant, he was a product of the Hastings Street neighborhood, and acted as Purple Gang Leader Abe Bernstein's bodyguard and driver before being sent up for murder.

Joe Miller, known as "Honey" because of his early employment as gunman in the Oakland Sugar House Gang, was a lamster from the Ohio area. He had been involved in the murder of a police officer during a liquor dispute. Wanted in Ohio under his real name, Salvatore Mirogliotta, "Honey" Miller became one of the few non-Jewish associates of the Purple Gang.

Abe Zussman, aka "Abie the Agent" after a popular Detroit Times comic strip, was a professional killer.

Zussman acted as an agent for several prominent bootleggers during Prohibition, placing their liquor in underworld resorts. He was rumored to have enjoyed his work so much that he would occasionally kill someone as a favor to a friend, free of charge.

Movie houses of the era began installing theater seats with metal backs possibly due to Zussman, who liked to work with a knife. He would follow a victim into a darkened theater, take a seat directly behind them until a noisy scene and run his knife through the back of the chair. When the movie ended and the house attendants tried to wake the "sleeper," they would find a body instead.

The balance of the gang: Isadore Kaminsky, Sam Bernstein, Lou Fleisher, Lou Gellerman, Jacob Levites, Ben Marcus, and John Wolff, were involved in a litany of similarly brutal activities as strong arm men and hijackers. Hijacking liquor from older and better established Detroit mobs earned the Purple's reputation for daring, ruthlessness, and ferocity.

The Bernstein Brothers

Joe and Raymond Bernstein were to become important leaders in the Purple Gang. Joe almost always dabbled in legitimate businesses. At one time he had owned a barber shop which was located on the present site of the Fox Theater in downtown Detroit. In later years Joe would be the owner of a men's clothing store, an automotive parts company, gambling casinos in Mexico, and oil wells in the Mt. Pleasant, Michigan area, with a lifelong friend named Sam Garfield. Joe would prosper as a consequence of his investments in the oil business. He would distance himself from the Purples in later years as the result of his success in legitimate business. During the mid– to late twenties, he was actively involved in the operations of the Oakland Sugar House and Purple Gangs. It was then that he built the bankroll that would eventually help financelegitimateenterprises.RaymondBernsteinstarted out with a powerful underworld gambler and resort owner named Joe Murphy. He later worked as a guard and a dealer in the Detroit area gambling dens. His blind pig, known as the "Kibbutzer Club," was located on the east side of Woodward Avenue at Columbia in downtown Detroit.

Both Joe and Ray Bernstein had grown up with the young mobsters associated with the Oakland Sugar House Gang and were close friends and business associates of many of these men. By the mid-twenties both Joe and Ray, as well as many other Purples, were spending as much time working their own individual rackets as they did with the Oakland Sugar House business. It was during this period that Joe Bernstein began to muscle in on the thriving Detroit area handbook rackets, over which the Bernstein brothers would eventually gain considerable control. During the late twenties Joe Bernstein would also be loosely linked to the narcotics racket by Federal authorities.

The Sam Lerner Case

Sugar House mobsters often picked up additional income by extorting money out of both legitimate and illegitimate neighborhood businesses. The Sam Lerner case is a typical example of the type of strong arm extortion practiced by the various ethnic underworld gangs of that time against business people within their ethnic communities. This extortion attempt had probably been the scheme of Harry Fleisher, Phil Keywell, and Sam "Gorilla" Davis. The four men originally arrested were Harry Fleisher, John Wolff (bookkeeper for the Oakland Sugar House business), Sam "Gorilla" Davis, and Isadore Kaminsky aka "Uncle." These men were formally charged with extorting $25 a week from Sam Lerner for a period of three weeks. Sam Lerner was the President of Michigan Millwork and Lumber Company.

Why Sam Lerner became an extortion victim of the Sugar House mobsters is not known. There had been a rumor circulating at that time that Lerner was operating a 30-gallon still in his lumber yard to supplement his income. He may have been buying his brewing supplies from the Oakland Sugar House.

The original arrest warrants were later expanded to include Charles Leiter, Philip Keywell, and two unknown persons, i.e., Richard Roe and John Doe, legal pseudonyms used by the Court to describe unidentified people in a legal warrant.

On April 23, 1928, Fleisher, Wolff, Kaminsky, and Davis were arraigned on charges of extortion. The following day Sam Lerner, accompanied by his wife and a police guard, appeared in front of Judge Thomas M. Cotter and identified the four men as having been involved in the extortion plot. That evening a man later identified as Sam Potasnik visited Lerner at his home. Potasnik, a Sugar House associate, warned Lerner that he would be killed if he pressed the extortion case. Lerner had two choices. If he wanted to live, he could repudiate his previous testimony or leave town. Sam Potasnik was later arrested as the result of his threat to Lerner and held for Obstruction of Justice.

On April 25, 1928, Lerner appeared at the hearing of the four men and begged Assistant Wayne County Prosecutor James Chenot and Judge Cotter to drop the extortion case. When Judge Cotter discovered that Lerner's life had been threatened he became infuriated. Fleisher, Wolff, Davis, and Kaminsky were immediately held for trial by Cotter under a bond of $10,000 each. Lerner eventually agreed to stay on and testify at the trial.

Thiseventwasoccurringatthesametimethat Charles Jacoby, vice president of Jacoby's French Cleaners and Dyers, and ten associates of the Oakland Sugar House Gang, now being called Purple Gangsters by the local press, were indicted and held for trial on charges of extortion. The extortion charge was based on the bombings, beatings, and murder perpetrated against various Detroit area cleaning and dying plants and their employees over the previous three years. This period of labor strife in the Detroit cleaning and dying industry would become known as the "Cleaners and Dyers War," and the case against the extortionists would culminate in the so-called "Purple Gang Trial" of 1928.

It is likely that the confusion between the Purple Gang and the Oakland Sugar House Gangs began during this period. Both were essentially the same organization. In the Sam Lerner case, one paper stated that Lerner had claimed that he "was not afraid of the Purple Gang and that he would not run away from them." In other newspaper articles, defendants Fleisher, Davis, Kaminsky, and Wolff are identified as members of the Oakland Sugar House Gang.

According to erroneous information supplied to the Detroit press by the self-proclaimed nemesis of the

Purple Gang, Inspector Henry J. Garvin, the Purples had taken over the Sugar House operation. Garvin blamed the recent spurt in extortion attempts on the gangsters' desire to develop a defense fund to cover legal costs incurred by the Purple gangster defendants in the Cleaners and Dyers extortion case. In an article in the *Detroit Free Press* edition of April 21, 1928, Garvin is quoted as saying that "the Oakland Sugar House mobsters were shaking down prosperous businessmen in the community to pay them tribute under threat of death, their strong arm methods going unpunished as the result of [the public's] general fear . . . to testify in court against these men."

There is no existing evidence that would suggest that the money extorted from local businessmen had ever been used by the gang to pay legal defense fees in the Purple Gang case. By this time the names of Sugar House gangsters and Purple gangsters seemed to become interchangeable in the local press. The Oakland gang had existed several years before the local newspapers began to refer to the underworld group as the Purple Gang.

In reality the Sugar House mob was not a separate group of gangsters taken over by the Purple Gang, but was comprised of many of the same mobsters that would be lumped under the general heading of the Purple Gang by the Detroit press. This confusion probably led writers in later years to conclude that the Oakland Sugar House Gang and Purple Gang were rival underworld organizations when, in fact, they were just different factions of the same underworld alliance of gangsters.

The original criminal complaint in the Sam Lerner extortion case had accused the defendants of threatening Sam Lerner by promising, "You pay us twenty-five dollars a week or we will kill you."

The preliminary hearing of the Lerner case was held in the courtroom of Recorders Court Judge Thomas M. Cotter on April 30, 1928. Sam Lerner was first questioned by Wayne County Assistant Prosecutor James E. Chenot. Lerner explained that he managed a lumber yard and that he knew all of the defendants. He had sold some lumber to a friend named Isadore Seligman.

While he was talking with Seligman, a man named Maurice Solomon had stopped by Seligman's house and asked to speak to Lerner. Solomon, who managed a tire store at the corner of Oakland and Holbrook Avenues in Detroit, told Lerner that several men, including a man later identified as Sam "Gorilla" Davis, were looking for Lerner and had threatened to kill him. Solomon suggested to Lerner that he should come back with him to the tire store and get a look at the gangsters who had been hanging around the shop earlier. Lerner told the court that he had gone back to the tire store with Solomon.

As Lerner walked into the garage he noticed Sam Davis talking to one of the employees. In Lerner's testimony he claimed that he had overheard the "Gorilla" say "if Sam Lerner makes a wrong move he is going to get it plenty tonight!" Lerner had noticed the handle of a pistol sticking out of Sam Davis's pocket. Davis then left the tire store without saying anything directly to Lerner and joined two other men who pulled up in a car. Lerner told the court that he had then walked up to the corner to see which way the men had gone when the car turned onto Oakland Avenue. He saw the car proceed north on Oakland and drive into the Sugar House. It was at this point that Lerner said he realized that he was dealing with members of the Oakland Sugar House Gang.

Lerner decided to go to the sugar warehouse and talk to Charlie Leiter and Henry Shorr, whom he knew to be the leaders of the mob, to try to find out why the gang had wanted to kill him and try to straighten things out. Before Lerner went over to the Sugar House he stopped at his friend, Isadore Seligman's home and borrowed Seligman's pistol to take along with him, because by this time, he had explained to the court, he was terrified.

By the time that Lerner walked into the Oakland Sugar House it was 4:15 in the afternoon. He stated to the court that when he walked into the building he noticed the gang's bookkeeper, Jack Wolff, sitting at a desk near the front of the warehouse. Harry Fleisher sat reading a newspaper. Sam Davis was also present. Lerner asked Wolff if he could speak to either Charlie Leiter or Henry Shorr. He was told that Shorr was in New York and that Leiter was out. Lerner told the court that he had asked the stranger who was sitting with Fleisher if he might have some idea where Leiter could be found. Lerner was directed to a restaurant across Oakland Avenue opposite the Sugar House.

Lerner walked over to the restaurant where he found Charlie Leiter, Leiter's wife, and two other men eating dinner. He explained to Leiter that Davis had threatened him and that he was trying to find out why the mob was after him. Lerner claimed that Leiter had asked him if he was carrying a gun. When Lerner admitted that he was armed, Leiter suggested that he go and kill Davis. Lerner told Leiter that he was not afraid to fight one or even two men but he did not want to do battle with the whole gang.

Lerner was terrified by this time, and told Leiter that he did not want any trouble, he just wanted to get things sorted out. Leiter then asked Lerner to give him his gun. When Lerner refused, Leiter then suggested that they both go over to the Sugar House and try to straighten things out. Lerner then followed Leiter out of the restaurant across Oakland Avenue and back into the sugar warehouse. When the two men entered the building Leiter told Lerner to wait outside his (Leiter's) office. Leiter then went into the office for a private conversation with Harry Fleisher. Suddenly, Fleisher lunged out of the office door with what Lerner would later describe as a black, automatic pistol, pushed it into Lerner's belly, and said, "Give me your gun, you son of a bitch, or I'm going to kill you." Lerner, who was frozen with fear, slowly handed Fleisher his pistol.

Fleisher then pushed his pistol harder into Lerner's stomach and pulled the trigger. Lerner held his breath as he heard the trigger fall on an empty chamber. He was now thoroughly terrorized. About this time Phil Keywell walked into the Sugar House. Leiter called Fleisher and Keywell into his office. Lerner would later claim that he saw the three men go into a huddle and that he had overheard Leiter say, "Let him square up with the boys and let him live." Fleisher and Keywell then came out and suggested to Lerner that they accompany him back to his friend Seligman's house to protect him and to have Lerner point out where he had seen Sam "Gorilla" Davis when he had threatened to kill Lerner. Fleisher then told Sam Lerner that he knew the men who wanted to kill him. Fleisher had then unloaded Lerner's pistol and handed it back to him.

Lerner testified that later that same evening a man

who gave his name as William Bernstein had stopped by the lumber yard. Whether William Bernstein was in reality one of the four Bernstein brothers is not known. Bernstein, who was a stranger to Lerner, told him that he had learned of his trouble with the Sugar House Gangsters and asked if he could be of any help in resolving the problem. Bernstein offered to play the role of mediator between Sam Lerner and the Sugar House mob. This incident represented a very similar scenario to the way that the Italian and Sicilian Black Handers extorted money from the businessmen in their community—first a death threat, then a mysterious mediator appears to straighten out the problem—the mediator all along being a member of the extortion gang himself.

Bernstein drove Sam Lerner back over to the Sugar House in what Lerner would later describe as a black Ford sedan at about 8:00 that evening. Bernstein formally introduced Lerner to Harry Fleisher and Phil Keywell and said that "these are the boys who he could straighten things out with." Sam Lerner testified that before Bernstein introduced him to Fleisher and Keywell the two mobsters had seemed to be reluctant to talk business with him. Once Bernstein had spoken to them they immediately let Lerner know exactly what they wanted. Fleisher explained to Lerner that he and Keywell needed a little money. When Lerner asked them how much they needed, they suggested that Lerner give as much as he could. Lerner told the two men that he was much too frightened to think straight that evening and asked if he could meet them the following afternoon at 1:00 at the Sugar House to make his first extortion payment.

Later that evening Lerner got into an argument with

Isadore Kaminsky alias "Uncle," another Sugar House gangster, over the extortion demands. Both Kaminsky and Lerner belonged to the fraternal organization, the Knights of Pythias. Lerner told Kaminsky that he thought it was appalling that a fellow fraternity brother would refuse to help him with his trouble. Kaminsky, unmoved by Lerner's plea for help, had simply replied "You'll have to straighten it out with the boys."

The next day, when Lerner went back to the Sugar House to negotiate with the gang he met Phil Keywell. Before long Harry Fleisher arrived. Lerner told the court that he had agreed to pay the two men $25 a week at that time and $25 immediately. Lerner stated that he had formalized this agreement with Jack Wolff whom he knew to be the gang's bookkeeper. He then gave Phil Keywell a check for $15 and $10 in cash. Lerner agreed to meet the men weekly at Isadore Seligman's home to make the extortion payments.

Rather than go to Seligman's home the following Saturday to make his payment, Lerner went to the Sugar House in an attempt to talk to Henry Shorr and possibly resolve the problem. Shorr had since gotten back into town from New York. When Lerner explained to Shorr what had happened Shorr gave Lerner a choice. Lerner testified that Shorr had said that he could call Phil Keywell and work something out with him or that he would personally go with Lerner to Detroit Police Headquarters to file a formal complaint. Shorr had then made a phone call according to Lerner, supposedly to police headquarters. Lerner thought that whoever Shorr had talked to suggested that Shorr bring Lerner down to Inspector Garvin's office at police headquarters.

Garvin was the head of the Detroit Police Department's Crime and Bomb Squad. This squad had gone by several different names as it evolved. It was first known as the "Black Hand" Squad, created, as the name implies, to deal with the "Black Hand" extortion gangs of that period. During the twenties the squad was renamed and reorganized as the Crime and Bomb Squad, and later as the Special Investigations Squad. The main duty of the Crime and Bomb Squad was to combat the organized and growing mobs of the Prohibition era Detroit underworld.

Inspector Garvin had risen rapidly in rank within the Detroit Police Department. Appointed to the force in 1914, he had been promoted to Inspector by 1927. At 37 years of age, Garvin was the youngest man ever to hold the rank of Inspector within the Detroit Police up to that time. His meteoric rise through the ranks was not without controversy.

There is evidence which tends to suggest that Inspector Garvin may have had a peculiar relationship with the Purple Gang. The first question that comes to mind is: why would a known mobster, a man identified as one of the leaders of both the Oakland Sugar House and Purple Gangs, suggest to one of the gang's extortion victims that he see a Police Inspector to file a complaint against gang members, and then accompany the victim to police headquarters? There would be other examples over the years of what appeared to be some kind of collusion between Garvin and various Purple mobsters.

According to Lerner, when Henry Shorr picked him and his wife up at Isadore Seligman's home he brought with him two men who identified themselves as detectives. They all drove to Detroit Police Headquarters together. When they arrived it was discovered that

Inspector Garvin was out. A week later Lerner filed his complaint with the Prosecutor's Office and the whole thing ended up in court.

The case against Charles Leiter was dismissed by Judge Cotter due to lack of evidence, a well-worn phrase. The court held Fleisher, Kaminsky, Davis, Keywell, and Jack Wolff over to stand trial in the Lerner case. The five men were found guilty of attempted extortion and placed on probation. This sentence was little short of amazing considering that by 1928 most of these men had lengthy police records.

Hijacking was a jackpot for organized crime. The rampant killings of anyone with a load of liquor was the risk incurred by independent rum-running. Men and sometimes women were routinely attacked by well-armed and organized gangs of hijackers like the Purple Gang. The independent operator in the rum-running business was fair game for both the U.S. Coast Guard and hijacking gangs, so by the later twenties organized crime in Detroit forced most independent rumrunners out of business.

The Purple Gang was broken down into factions, according to their services. The Little Jewish Navy was the one that ran stolen liquor from Canada in several privately owned speedboats. Almost all of the Purples' liquor was stolen from some other gang.

Local distributors for hijacked liquor were a rare find for a gang. One early distributor was a hard-boiled import, a St. Louis gangster known as Johnny Reid, who's 1926 murder brought the Purple Gang into an alliance that led them into dominance.

Chapter *3*

The Murder of Johnny Reid

"A power to be reckoned with was the slight, almost frail Reid, but his removal from the underworld with a charge of hot lead . . . will not by any means bring about an armistice in the guerrilla warfare that has made the staccato of gunfire a familiar sound in . . . Detroit."

—Anonymous

The liquor hijacked by the Purple Gang presented a problem of distribution. They'd found a valuable partner when they arranged to have the stolen cache dispersed by Johnny Reid.

Reid was active in the underworlds of Missouri, Illinois, and now Detroit. He was closely associated with the Egan's Rats gang of St. Louis and counted among his friends notorious gunmen like Ezra Milford Jones and Fred "Killer" Burke. He had probably been attracted to Detroit by Prohibition, for its opportunity to make an easy black market buck.

Reid's former friends, the Rats, produced some of the toughest bank robbers and gunmen of the twentieth century. His move to Detroit introduced out-of-state gangsters to the Purple Gang, providing killers happy to lend their talents to Reid's new colleagues. With imported gunmen, identification was difficult and the source of gang wars untraceable.

Police knew Reid from 1919 when he was arrested for murder after an argument over a woman, but released for lack of evidence. He then became involved in a second romantic triangle and was shot four times in the head while visiting the woman. For all of his dangerous associations, women seemed to be Reid's greatest weakness.

After several months he recovered quite miraculously in a New York hospital but lost sight in his left eye. A diminutive, frail man, he was nonetheless a fearless and dangerous adversary. The fact that he recovered at all enhanced his reputation as the veteran of many gang wars.

He began to employ the ferocious Purple Gangsters as bodyguards and bouncers. Eddie Fletcher, a prize fighter turned Purple and rising star in the mid twenties underworld, became Reid's personal bodyguard. They developed a friendship that developed into a relationship between Reid and the Purple Gang.

Unbeknownst to the underworld, Reid's role in the Purple Gang's rise to power began with his gathering a gang of kidnappers who would wreak havoc throughout the underworld. He originated the idea of kidnapping other racketeers. The rationale was that wealthy gamblers and racketeers could be kidnapped quietly and would pay for their freedom, for fear of drawing attention.

In an ironic twist, most members of kidnapping gangs of the late twenties had been imported to Detroit by the same gamblers and wealthy racketeers that would become their victims. It all goes to show that life is short in organized crime and everyone eventually meets his nemesis. Reid's was Mike Dipisa.

Mike Dipisa had arrived from Chicago in 1923. He wasted no time establishing a ruthless reputation in Detroit, guarding gambling parlors. He branched out into other crimes but was always released for lack of evidence. Witnesses felt that a memory lapse was better than a trip to the bottom of the Detroit River.

For several years Dipisa was one of the most shot at characters in the Detroit underworld, yet amazingly he had never been hit. Even close friends of Dipisa were afraid to take a walk with him in public for fear they'd go down during an attack on Mike.

In June of 1925 an incident occurred which demonstrated one of Mike Dipisa's stronger personality traits— he was a coward. Dipisa and several of his men held up a Detroit bookmaker named Jacob Fricker. In the days following the robbery Dipisa was frequently shot at when he drove down the street.

Taking these assassination attempts as a hint that he held up the wrong man, he quickly messengered back all of Fricker's stolen valuables. Dipisa's reputation was badly bruised.

Dipisa knew Reid's reputation as a tough character. As a crime leader, he nonetheless would get personally involved in rum feuds and did not run from confrontation. Dipisa selected Reid as an extortion target because if Reid could be made to give in to Dipisa's extortion demands his reputation would be repaired, other blind pig operators would pay.

The confrontation between Dipisa and Reid began in August of 1926. One hot afternoon, three men from the Dipisa mob entered Reid's blind pig and announced that Mike Dipisa wanted a cut of the profits. They dared Reid to do something about it.

Reid threw the men out. Furious, he contacted some of his friends from Egan's Rats Mob, a gang that still held great power in St. Louis, and had nothing to fear in Detroit.

Reid specifically called in Fred "Killer" Burke, a professional bank robber; and Milford Jones, a professional killer. Six gunmen arrived, maintained a low profile, and began watching Mike Dipisa. The first confrontation took place shortly thereafter.

Reid and his gunmen were cruising the streets in Reid's big touring car, visiting Dipisa's favorite blind pigs, restaurants, and gambling houses. When the gunmen finally spotted Dipisa in a high-powered roadster they started shooting. Two police officers walking a beat saw a dozen shots fired while the cars raced side by side. Amazingly, nobody was wounded. As the cars disappeared around the corner the patrolmen commandeered a taxi and raced after the gangsters. Dipisa's car was forced to the curb and searched but by then no guns were found.

All three denied they fired. Dipisa, true to the underworld code of silence, said they'd been attacked for no reason. He appeared shaken by the savagery of the attack. It had all been too much for Mike Dipisa.

When a second attack followed, he finally sent peace envoys to Johnny Reid. A temporary truce was called and a meeting arranged. Dipisa denied that he sent men to strong-arm Reid, and claimed there had been a misunderstanding.

In the ultimate act of gangland cowardice, Dipisa told Reid that the gunmen were not his men. According to underworld informers, he denied involvement with his own friends to save himself. The next day their bodies were found in some weeds.

Reid had driven a hard bargain. He would only agree to a truce if Dipisa would produce the men he claimed were responsible, so that Reid could dispense his own justice. One of the men had gone into hiding, but the other two were given up and lured to Reid's blind pig.

When police arrived on the scene one had lived just long enough to tell police that they'd been shot by Johnny Reid. When Reid denied any knowledge and police found no evidence, he was released. Feeling vindicated, Reid allowed Dipisa an uneasy truce.

But if Reid was enjoying Mike Dipisa's discomfort, it was to be short-lived. Early one morning in December of 1926, Reid pulled into the parking lot of his apartment building and as he came to a stop, a gunman with a sawed-off shotgun stepped out of the shadows and fired. The force of the shot in the back of Reid's head threw his body into the windshield, killing him instantly.

The murder was reported when a passerby noticed blood on the running board. The killer was nowhere to be found. More importantly, in the eyes of the Purple Gang, their most valuable distributor was gone with the death of Johnny Reid, and someone had to pay.

The rumor that Mike Dipisa had hired a Chicago gunman for the execution spurred the gang on. The identity of the gunman was learned and Reid's murder avenged. It sent a valuable message about how even distant connections to the gang were protected to the death.

The Purple Gang was now allied with the cream of

Egan's Rats mob. Reid had brought in Fred Burke, Milford Jones, and other Egan's Rats to freelance as executioners for Detroit gangs. In his death, his Rats friends shared a cause with his Purple friends that put them into business together.

The Purple Gang became twice as powerful as any other Detroit gang with Egan's Rats by their side. Mike Dipisa was feeling powerful too. He had the last word in his feud with Reid, spoken through the business end of a shotgun.

The gangster world thought Mike Dipisa led a charmed life and that bullets would never be the cause of his demise. For several years he was one of the most shot at characters in the Detroit underworld, yet amazingly had never been hit. Even close friends of Dipisa were afraid to take a walk with him, but his luck ran out less than two years after the murder of Johnny Reid.

In 1928, Dipisa up to his old tricks, sent one of his musclemen to a blind pig to extort profits. Police were told two versions of what transpired that night. One was that the thug walked into the blind pig and made the "business proposal," at which point he was slapped in the face and told to go back and tell what he'd gotten for his trouble.

The other story was that the thug had been sitting in his car waiting for the blind pig owner. The owner arrived and accidently bumped Dipisa's thug while parking. The two men argued and, incredibly, the strong arm man sent to intimidate was knocked down by the owner.

According to both versions the embarrassed thug, Zanetti, left and returned with Mike Dipisa to help him save face. Unknown to Dipisa and Zanetti, a constable named Edward McPherson was sitting in the blind pig waiting to serve it a summons. In his statement to Detroit police, McPherson explained that when Dipisa and Zanetti returned to the blind pig Dipisa asked the owner to step outside.

McPherson crouched inside the blind pig's door, gun drawn. They argued outside, and Dipisa and Zanetti fired five shots at point blank range. McPherson rushed out and the gunfight was on. Suddenly one man fell—it was Mike Dipisa. The impossible to hit gangster had finally been gunned down, defeated by an argument over his embarrassed thug.

Dipisa's funeral was one of the first lavish gangster funerals in Detroit. Eight cars filled with flowers followed the hearse to Mt. Olivet Cemetery after a high mass. Attended by Detroit's most prominent racketeers, the mile long funeral procession was preceded by a 15-piece band which played dirges all the way to the cemetery.

Although a bit of a clown in the underworld, Dipisa did order the killing of Reid that brought together Egan's Rats and the Purple Gang. Ironically, his clumsy crimes created the monster that was the Purple Gang and its accomplices, Egan's Rats.

Rats member, Fred "Killer" Burke would go on to become the main talent in Detroit's first machine gun murders. These shootings took place in a building known as Milaflores Apartments, the site of the Prohibition Era's famous "Milaflores Massacre."

The unprecedented ruthlessness of Milaflores would guarantee the reputation of the Purple Gang in their aspirations to control Detroit.

Chapter 4

The Milaflores Apartment Massacre

"The machine gun worked, that's all I remember."

—Deathbed statement, Frank Wright, March 28, 1927

It was only 4:45 one March morning in 1927, when the tenants of the Milaflores Apartment Building were jolted out of their beds by the deafening roar of machine gun and pistol fire. For several moments all hell broke loose in the building. The last sounds were of shoes scraping down the back stairway into the alley, and the roar of an automobile engine into the morning darkness.

A deadly silence enveloped the building's corridors. No one dared look out their door.

Finally, one of the tenants on the third floor peered into the hallway. The air was still thick with the smell of burned gunpowder and cloudy with plaster that had been ripped from the walls by bullets.

Near the doorway of Apartment 308 lay three bullet-riddled bodies. Two had literally been cut to pieces by the machine gun fire. One man still seemed to be breathing shallowly.

Blood pooled into the hallway. The incident, dubbed the Milaflores Apartment Massacre, was now part of the bloody history of Detroit's gangland wars. The three victims were identified as Isaac Reisfield, William Harrison, and Frank Wright, all local gangsters.

Both Reisfield and Harrison were killed instantly. Frank Wright was still barely alive when police arrived. Wright and the two bodies were taken to the hospital, where attendants would comment that the bodies had so many bullet holes in them it was impossible to distinguish wounds.

The machine gun incident was without precedent. It predated the days when machine guns were almost a symbol of the underworld, the gangster's weapon of choice. It had not been illegal to own a machine gun in Michigan until the Massacre, but legislation was soon passed making ownership a crime.

Soon after the murder of Johnny Reid, it was rumored that one of the Milaflore victims, Frank Wright, had been hired to kill Johnny Reid. Whether or not Wright's contractor was Mike Dipisa is open to speculation. Typically a hired gunman was used in order to come in for one day, complete his contract, and leave the state to keep local police from solving the murder.

Wright had arrived in Detroit from Chicago in October of 1926, and, after killing Johnny Reid, stayed on. This was his first mistake. He made his services available to local gambling houses as a guard and gunman, where he met befriended fellow victims Isaac

Reisfield and William Harrison, that was their first mistake.

Frank was shaking down local gamblers for protection money. He probably preyed on gamblers protected by Purple Gangsters. This indiscretion as well as the murder of Johnny Reid, would easily have brought on the massacre.

The Purples devised a scheme to lure Frankie Wright to his death. Reisfield and Harrison merely went along to Milaflores that morning, and were in the wrong place at the wrong time. The Purples knew Wright's recently kidnapped business associate Meyer Bloomfield, was also a close friend and figured he'd be willing to meet with the kidnappers.

With his last breath, Frank Wright told everything. On the morning of March 28th, he received a phone call in his room at the Book Cadillac Hotel. His friend was being held in room 308 of the Milaflores Apartments and if he came to this address he could negotiate for his release.

Reisfield and Harrison heard Wright take the call and suspected a trap. They drove to Milaflores armed. When they arrived Wright rapped on the door to no answer.

As the three men turned to leave, the fire door at the end of the hallway burst open and erupted with gunfire. The ambush happened so fast that none of the men had a chance to pull their pistols.

Detroit homicide investigators would later trace Apartment 308 in the Milaflores complex to a Purple gangster. The crime scene unit found an arsenal of 12 pistols, dumdum bullets, three shotguns, and blackjacks. Items found in apartment 308 made it look like any number of people used the place.

When shown a wanted poster found in the rooms, the landlady identified Salvatore Mirogliotta as a man who frequently visited. She told police that Mirogliotta went by the name of Sam Miller, better known to police as Joe "Honey" Miller, a notorious gunman. It was obvious that the place was a base of operations.

But if this group had actually kidnapped Bloomfield, why would they have lured Wright and his associates to the front door of their own hideout for a murder?

The first break in the investigation was soon to come. At 2:00 A.M. on March 29th, police arrested two men. An automatic pistol and a revolver with extra ammunition for both were found in their vehicle. They gave their names as Harry Levine and Robert Burke.

Harry Levine turned out to be Purple Abe Axler. The other man was Thomas Camp, but it was the alias he'd first given that would make him infamous: Fred "Killer" Burke was the close friend and associate of the deceased Johnny Reid.

The massacre was the first time a machine gun had been used in such a depraved manner, and Fred "Killer" Burke's specialty was machine gun work. These events drew a direct connection between the Purple Gang, Fred "Killer" Burke, the murder of Johnny Reid and the Milaflores Massacre.

On the same day Axler and Burke were arrested Purple Gang associate Jules Jaffee was picked up in connection with the Milaflores slayings. The police received an anonymous tip that Jaffee knew something. Investigators had two days to produce evidence.

The judge could only continue to hold Axler and Burke for trial if something substantial was produced. When the habeas corpus review came before him no conviction worthy evidence had surfaced, and the two men were released. No one was ever brought to trial for the Milaflores apartment murders; to this day the crime remains officially unsolved.

The brutal murders of Wright, Reisfield, and Harrison rocked the Detroit underworld, marking a turning point in the evolution of the gang. As early as 1925 the Purples gained notoriety as hijackers, labor racketeers, and freelance gunmen, but the massacre made them. They proved themselves to be a cunning group with powerful allies, obviously ready to do anything to teach a lesson to whomever betrayed them.

The most notorious Egan's Rats affiliated with the Purples in order of nerve were Fred Burke, Isadore "Bubs" Londe, and Ezra Milford Jones. Isadore Londe was known for violent and sensational bank robberies executed in daylight as well as for his frequent use of submachine guns. His killings were simply depraved indifference.

Ezra Milford Jones ran many Italian and Sicilian gangsters out of St. Louis. These Mafioso in turn became powerful Detroit leaders by the late twenties. Jones carried a grudge, and so when they turned up in Detroit he began a personal feud with the Italian underworld.

According to rumor, he killed 29 Sicilian mobsters. Although Jones was a physically small, psychotic punk with schoolboy looks, he made up for his physical stature with ferocity. He would yell "Take it, Dago!" as he shot his victim down. Although unpredictable and greatly feared throughout the underworld, he was particularly hated by the Italians and was eventually murdered by the Mafia.

Their dossiers alone were enough for other gangs to submit to the Purples. Already ranked high on local and Federal Public Enemy lists, Burke was the icing on the cake. Within seven years he would help commit:

- Racketeer kidnappings in Detroit
- The John Kay Jewelry Robbery
- The holdup of the First National Bank of Indiana
- The St. Valentine's Day Massacre
- A mail truck robbery worth $200,000
- The United Railways Robbery
- The holdup of the Farmers and Merchants Bank of Wisconsin
- The holdup of the Farmers National Bank of Kentucky
- The holdup of the Lincoln National Bank & Trust Company

The above list of crimes is by no means complete or even representative of the many murders, robberies, and kidnappings in which he played a part. By the time of his final capture and life imprisonment Burke was considered America's most dangerous man.

By the mid-twenties, Egan's Rats and The Purples were consolidating their brute power. With Rats as gunmen, the Purple Gang tolerated no interlopers—including the police. The murder of Detroit Patrolman Vivian Welch crossed the shaky line between their criminal world and the authority outside of it.

Chapter 5

The Murder of Vivian Welch

"Welch was strictly on the shakedown. We have found that he made the rounds of many blind pigs and threatened to have them raided if they did not pay him . . . from what we have learned he got plenty. But he finally ran up against the wrong boys."

—Inspector Fred Frahm, February 4th, 1928

O n New Year's Day 1928, the future of Detroit Police Officer Vivian Welch could not have looked brighter. But by the end of January he would be found unconscious and near death, the victim of a gangland attack.

As a rookie, Welch had become friends with veteran police officer Max Whisman. The older man introduced Welch around the department and took him into his confidence: he had developed a racket. Officer Whisman was shaking down blind pig operators and bootleggers on his beat.

A raid could be very costly in terms of the loss of an operator's equipment when Prohibition officers busted it up. All Whisman had to do was threaten Prohibition violators with a police raid and the money rolled in. So, Whisman and Welch became partners in the protection business.

They were aware that bootleggers were protected by organized crime. Gangsters were quick to put their competitors out of business "permanently" as long as they were other gangsters, but never police. It was not considered good business to kill police, there was enough money for everybody.

Unfortunately for Whisman and Welch, this protocol was not embraced by the Purple Gang. Barely out of their teens in 1926 the purples were already fearsome, and did not adhere to codes. What gave them their edge was that anyone who crossed paths with them was fair game.

Whisman and Welch had begun to prosper but whispers of Whisman's extortion racket circulated throughout the Department. Oddly, Welch escaped suspicion. Amidst rumors Whisman resigned. The resignation took place presumably to protect his lucrative underworld shakedowns because after a cooling off period, Whisman was reinstated on the force and, still under suspicion, began making pickups on days off. He kept his distance from Welch during duty hours but the two remained partners in extortion.

Greed got the best of them, and they increased their payoff demands. Bitterness grew until a group of bootleggers actually complained to police about Whisman. There was no way to arrest them as the operators, predictably, wouldn't testify in court.

However, their complaints provided ammunition

for a police trial board to bring Whisman up on charges. He was officially discharged from the Detroit Police Force. Still, Welch was untouched.

The law had nothing left to say about what they were up to, but someone more powerful and infinitely more intimidating did. When Welch and Whisman shook down a Purple Gang operated brewery, Welch was singled out for vengeance. Detroit Police theorized that Whisman was forced by the Purples to set up his partner for them by driving him to his execution.

At 1:10 P.M. on a January day in 1928 a woman, startled by gunfire, rushed to her living room window. She saw a man limping through her yard, chased by two men firing pistols as they ran. They disappeared down the street and after several more shots, she heard the screech of tires.

Down the block, a second woman saw the man collapse in the street. One of the gunmen stood over the body and took careful aim, firing several rounds into his head as he lay prone. The woman wrote down the license plate of the getaway car and phoned police.

Information on his body identified the dead man as Vivian Welch. The attack was so blatant that many eyewitness accounts pieced together the events of the murder. Those present from the beginning related how the car stopped suddenly in the middle of the street and a man (Welch) jumped out and started running.

Two men then vaulted from the car with pistols, shooting as they ran. When the victim fell in the street, both men fired several rounds into him. They turned around the car and passed right over the body as they roared away.

Arrests in the police dragnet ranged from every

known Purple to Whisman and his common law wife, whose alibis didn't match. Whisman told police he arrived home around noon the day of the murder and left again at 3 P.M. She said he'd not returned until four, which would've given him time to set Welch up for the attack.

In addition to the gangsters taken in the dragnet, police arrested six Purples by February 2nd. Blind pig operator Ben Weiss was booked on the murder charge, and Whisman was closely watched. Police felt he was at least present for the murder.

All were booked under their aliases and sent around the loop while the police scrambled desperately for leads. After travelling through every Detroit precinct house, they ended up at police headquarters. Whisman was being held on a technical charge of homicide.

In the meantime, Vivian Welch was being given a hero's funeral accompanied by a police marching band. Police were unable to connect him to any crimes because his record appeared clean. The prosecutor made a statement to the Detroit press that he believed the actual murderers of Welch were now in police custody.

On February 4th Police Inspector Frahm, Prosecutor Chenot, and Commissioner Rutledge told Detroit press that Welch was definitely not killed in the line of duty. They revealed that Welch and Whisman extorted money from blind pigs, and that Welch was killed as a result. It was a bold move by high ranking officials increasingly tired of protecting criminals.

The original nine suspects arrested were released on writs of habeas corpus and then re-arrested the same evening on suspicion of murder, due to evidence supposedly discovered by corrupt Inspector Henry J. Garvin. Gangleader Abe Bernstein was actually handcuffed leaving the Court Building on his writ of habeas corpus.

Ten minutes after the arrest, Bernstein's lawyer served another writ of habeas corpus that demanded Abe be produced before the Judge. He was released on a bond of $10,000 the following day. In the twenties, a good defense lawyer was as essential to a gangster as his favorite gun.

The Prosecutor went to the press, describing Abe Bernstein as organizer and leader of the Purple Gang who provided hired guns to underworld operators in need of protection. By going public about organized crime in Detroit the Prosecutor was declaring war. The drastic police crackdown was the only positive consequence of the murder of Vivian Welch.

The Detroit underworld was on guard. To gun down a cop in broad daylight as the Purples had was the ultimate ruthless act of protection of a gang's interests. One that had been executed with total indifference to the authority of the police. No one ever went to trial for Vivian Welch's murder.

The killing enhanced the Purple Gang's reputation for retaliation and for their untouchable veneer. It also proved that even law enforcement officers could become targeted by the Purples if they thought that they were being crossed. The spectacular execution occurred at a significant point in the Purple Gang's evolution.

For several years a trade war had been raging in the cleaning and dying industry. It cost local businessmen hundreds of thousands of dollars in plant damage and resulted in the murder of at least two union officials.

Now officially the hardest, harshest gang to hire,

the Purples began a reign of terror in the cleaning industry. They were hired as muscle for a racketeer-oper-
ated trade organization called the Wholesale Cleaners
and Dyers Association. By the war's bloody end the
gang would be revealed as more than just muscle.

Francis X. Martel, the Detroit Federation of Labor
President, persuaded independent shops to join the
Wholesale Cleaners and Dyers union, and those who
declined suffered the consequences that a visit by the
Purples could bring. Abe Bernstein, his brother-in-law
Charles Jacoby, and Francis Martel were secretly partners from the start. The trade war would finally culminate in a Purple Gang extortion trial that would be the
first serious legal threat to their power.

Chapter *6*

The Cleaners and Dyers War

"Rounded up and waiting for trial, are a bunch of Jacoby's terrorists, the so called 'Purple Gang.' It is now up to the Prosecutor and the courts to go to the very bottom of this case and exterminate for all time this vicious gang and its influence."

—Police Commissioner
William Rutledge, April 10th, 1928

"I never heard of an organization of businessmen where men with guns would come around and collect dues."

—Judge John M. Cotter

One night in early spring of 1928 a local doctor turned into his driveway only to discover someone had parked across it. Irritated, he put the sedan in neutral and pushed it out of the way with his car. In the darkness, he never noticed the blood soaked body lying inside.

53

On the floor against the back seat was the body of Samuel Polakoff, vice president of the Union Cleaners and Dyers Company of Detroit. More importantly he was the representative of the Wholesale Cleaners and Dyers Association, and the last man in the 1925 trade war to be "taken for a ride." A coroner's examination of the body revealed he'd been beaten to death with a hammer.

The signifigance of Polakoff's murder was that it finally broke the code of silence that enabled the Purples to dominate the cleaners and dyers for so long. Fearing for their lives, ten cleaning plant operators went to the police to explain the reason for the killing. Polakoff was so high profile that the Purples obviously didn't care who they eliminated, any one of them could have been next.

They told police that there were twenty other independent Cleaners and Dyers who had been harassed by death threats and bombings, and blamed the situation on Jacoby and the Purple Gang. Detroit police did not realize at the time that the suspects in custody for Sam Polakoff's murder were the gang's most dangerous men.

The arrests culminated in the trial that not only ended the Cleaners and Dyers War, but exposed organized crime's pivotal role in the famous labor conflict.

Before organized crime took over, the cleaning industry was a straightforward business plagued by price wars. It was comprised of many large scale wholesale cleaning plants that performed all the cleaning and dyeing functions for retail tailor shops.

A group of independent laundry drivers, known in the business as Commission Men, picked up clothing at tailor shops, transported it to central cleaning plants and then brought it back to the shops. They worked for wholesalers as well as private clientele. On commission they averaged at least $300 per week, a strong wage for the twenties.

The inside workers worked in the plants cleaning, dyeing, and pressing the clothing. They were the bulk of the cleaning labor force. The third group in the industry were the Retail Tailors.

In early 1924, a price war raged between wholesale cleaning plants driving down industry prices. Most of the large wholesalers were losing money. Retail tailors avoided cleaning bills by merely switching their business to another plant.

The situation was ripe for a labor racketeer to step in and gain control of the industry's unions. He appeared in the form of Chicago union organizer and labor racketeer Ben Abrams. The idea of making the cleaning and dyeing industry into a racket began in Chicago, with a group of labor racketeers who'd infiltrated labor unions in order to manipulate the cleaning and dyeing industry.

A writer of the era described that city's cleaning and dyeing racket as a "collusive agreement" or a racket that grew out of the greed of legitimate businessmen, labor leaders, and the underworld.

A "collusive agreement" was the hardest racket to expose. Respectable businessmen were part of it, and when it came under scrutiny the principals hid behind legitimate business institutions. In the Cleaners and Dyers War the legitimate business institution was the Detroit Federation of Labor.

Ben Abrams was affiliated with the American Federation of Labor. Frank X. Martel, President of the Detroit Federation of Labor, called upon Abrams to come to Detroit to "organize" the cleaning business. At one point, Ben Abrams and another Chicago labor racketeer were actually arrested by Detroit police.

They were charged with carrying concealed weapons and by way of explanation, they came right out and said they were in the city because there was a lot of money to be made in the labor racket. They even offered to cut the police in on their profits! Both had lengthy Chicago police records for labor related murders—yet in true underworld fashion they were protected from on high.

The first attempts to unionize the cleaning and dyeing industry were unsuccessful, but in the spring of 1925 Abrams suggested that the wholesalers form an association to control industry prices. Within three weeks, the largest Detroit area cleaning plants were members of the newly formed Wholesale Cleaners and Dyers Association.

All unions were affiliated with the Frank X. Martel-headed Detroit Federation of Labor. Chicago leader Abrams promised a general price increase to end price wars if the cleaners and dyers got together and unionized their plants.

Detroit cleaners and dyers would soon realize what they had gotten themselves into. At a meeting of the Laundry Drivers Union Frank Martel and a Chicago labor organizer explained what happened in Chicago with cleaners who got out of line, describing plant bombings, beatings, the theft of full laundry trucks, and worse for recalcitrant union members.

When the newly formed Inside Workers union demanded shorter hours and time-and-a-half for overtime, Martel prevented them from getting their demands. As a reward, the Wholesale Cleaners and Dyers Association gave Martel seven hundred dollars. The "gift" would eventually tie Martel to Association payoffs during his trial.

Soon after the industry was organized, wholesalers held a meeting and decided that the tailors could not switch their business from one cleaning plant to another without a good reason. A board was set up to review requests from retail tailors to switch cleaning plants. The new review board was comprised of a representative from the wholesale cleaners, retail tailors, and the drivers unions. On the surface, conditions in the cleaning and dyeing industry seemed to improve.

Abrams was ready to step out of the picture. When he left, he was given $1500 from the Wholesale Cleaners and Dyers Association for organizing the trade. Charles Jacoby Jr., brother-in-law of Purple Gangster Abe Bernstein, was named by Abrams as the only wholesale cleaner with whom he would deal directly. During this time, Martel and Charles Jacoby worked toward establishing the new prices and policies of the newly unionized cleaning industry.

Jacoby became the Association's first President and Frank Martel received a share of union dues. Initially the dues of the Wholesalers Union were $25 a week. This changed to 2% of each wholesale cleaning plant's gross business.

After the industry was "organized," Martel was constantly requesting donations to what he called the "construction fund." It was supposed to sponsor pickets and pay for the advertising costs of the Association. In reality, the money was spent to finance Purple Gang terrorism used against independent plants who refused to join the Association.

One such independent was the Retail Tailors. When

the Wholesalers Association doubled cleaning prices, Retail Tailors became outraged. One night in the summer of 1925, they called a meeting at the Detroit Labor Temple to protest the new price structure. Frank Martel presided, with a brick in his hand. When a tailor made an attempt to stand up and protest the price structure, Martel slammed the brick down on the table and screamed, "Shut up and sit down, if you know what's good for you!"

Anyone who raised questions at future union meetings had trouble around their shops. Bricks destroyed plant windows at night and shops were stench bombed— a practice which ruined thousands of dollars worth of clothing. It was the beginning of an industry-wide reign of terror.

Victims were businesses whose owners had the "wrong attitude" toward union organization. The violence steadily escalated into beatings, thefts, plant bombings, and murder. The Purple Gang and their associates were used right from the start to keep cleaners and tailors in line.

They changed from gambling operators, bodyguards and hijackers to union terrorists quite easily. They had already been shaking down underworld operators. Preying on legitimate businessmen was a logical next step, one that catapulted them into the upper echelon of organized crime.

Charles Jacoby Jr. was a key player in the conflict. His marriage to a sister of the Bernstein brothers was kept under wraps, so the Purple Gang's connection to the Cleaners and Dyers War remained vague. By the mid-twenties the Purples had developed such a reputation for savagery in dealing with enemies that victims in the cleaners and dyers war said nothing for fear for their lives. No one outside of the industry suspected the infiltration of organized crime.

The Purple Gang kept everyone's mouth shut through innovative terrorist techniques. Harry Rosman related, in the famous Purple Gang Trial, how the association used Purple Gang thugs to destroy his plant.

After his resignation from the Wholesale Cleaners Association, two men rapped on the door of his independent Famous Cleaners and Dyers Company. When the night watchman appeared they pulled guns and forced their way in. Without a word, they tied the terrified watchman to a post and began dumping gasoline over desktops and clothing.

They forced the guard into their car. As they pulled away, one tossed a lit cigarette lighter through the open door. The guard watched helplessly from the backseat as the building exploded into flames. The plant watchman was driven to the country, thrown out of the car and warned not to return to the plant.

The Purple's methods with uncooperative union members was equally violent. After a price increase in 1925, a group of retail tailors resigned from the union. The union rebels formed two cooperative cleaning plants, known as The Empire Cleaners and Dyers Company, and The Novelty Cleaners and Dyers Company.

At approximately 4:30 A.M. on October 26th, 1925 the neighborhood of the Novelty Cleaners and Dyers plant was rocked by a terrific explosion. Windows in nearby buildings were shattered and residents jarred out of sleep. When the smoke cleared, the Novelty plant was demolished.

Investigators would later discover a nitroglycerin bomb hidden in the plant. The Empire Cleaners and Dyers Company was also bombed that day. Eleven tailor shops had been stench bombed in the week prior to the destruction of the two plants.

A couple of months later the Association called a meeting to introduce its members to the Purple Gang. The Purples, waved their guns and warned the audience what might happen if they to decided to quit the organization as their unfortunate colleagues had done.

The Purple Gang was especially important at this meeting because the remaining members now owed even higher dues for their businesses. It was decided that to deal with the detractors the Association would charge members a weekly increase of 10% of their gross business, to fund a buy out of non-union plants. Not many protested—once the independent plants had been bombed, all the Purples had to do to convince a Wholesaler to get in line was to leave a stick of dynamite with a half-burned fuse at their plant door.

Intimidations built up so severely by 1928 that Samuel Polakoff's pummeled body opened the floodgates of powerful legitimate businessmen who'd been sucked too far into the underworld, who'd become more frightened of murder at the Gang's hands than of turning them in. The official charge was conspiracy to extort money and the warrant named Charles Jacoby Jr., Abe Bernstein, and eleven Purple Gangsters.

During the Purple Gang pretrial examination, a witness was asked if he knew why he had to pay dues and where the money was going. He stated that the money was for protection against plant fires, thefts, bombings, and beatings. He paid the dues to avoid problems with the Purple gang.

In addition to the blatant gangster intimidation, the trial would bring out adminstrative corruption previously known to only a few powerful players. When

Jacoby resigned from the union in 1927, it was suspected that he'd attempted to line up the commission
drivers against retail tailors and cleaning plants. At the
same time Jacoby's rival, Harry Rosman, started a
movement to eliminate commissions for drivers and
put them on straight salary, prompting many drivers
to quit their plants to side with Jacoby.

Any drivers remaining on Rosman's side were then
confronted by the Purples and threatened that if they
refused to work for Jacoby, "we don't know what will
happen to you!" According to one tailor, the labor
bosses were trying to divide the tailors and the drivers
because members were beginning to break away from
the Association's control.

Shortly after the commission drivers sided with
Jacoby, a message was delivered to Harry Rosman.
He was told that Jacoby had the power to eliminate
the commission drivers in exchange for $1000 a week.
At the next union meeting Jacoby attended with a committee of laundry drivers, introduced himself as business representative of the Drivers Union, and had a
vote taken wherein the commission drivers were eliminated.

Abe Bernstein then met with Rosman and told him
the Detroit cleaning industry would be straightened out
if Rosman paid him $1000 a week. Rosman refused
and suffered the aforementioned bombing of his Famous Cleaners and Dyers plant.

The union eventually agreed to pay Bernstein his
money to insure protection of their plants. It was raised
through contributions from each operator beyond the
ordinary weekly dues. At the next meeting, Jacoby
took the floor and announced that the only way he
would be a party to the agreement was if the Association

agreed to make Abe Bernstein boss.

Abe Bernstein then announced that he was going to "run the parade from now on and that it would be too bad for anyone who dropped out of line." Union members later testified that the organization paying Abe Bernstein and the cessation of all fires, bombings, and mayhem matched to the day.

After taking over the Wholesale Cleaners and Dyers Association, Abe Bernstein and a group of heavily armed Purple gangsters would appear promptly at the start of the weekly meetings. The gunmen would sit in an adjoining room while Bernstein opened the meeting, collected the dues, and left with his men.

When Charles Jacoby resigned from the Association, the dues increased. A member complained to Sam Polakoff, acting business representative, and was told that nothing could be done as the dues were set by Abe Bernstein and Charles Jacoby. The Association voted to take Bernstein off the payroll, Polakoff reluctantly agreed, and his murder is history.

When the operators filed formal complaints against Jacoby and the Purple Gang, Abe Bernstein, accompanied by attorney Edward Kennedy Jr., said he didn't understand what the commotion was all about. He claimed no knowledge of terrorism in the Detroit cleaning industry.

Inspector Henry J. Gravin was amused by Bernstein's claim that he was employed as a shoe salesman. According to Garvin, "The Bernstein boys never had any connection with the shoe business unless it was to wear out shoes running from the police!"

It appeared that the State had an airtight case against the Purple Gang on the Cleaners and Dyers War charges. The State contended that Charles Jacoby and the Purple Gang had attempted to destroy the business of members of the Detroit Wholesalers Association with terrorism. But immediately after the trial began, the State's case began to suffer setbacks.

❖❖❖

Two of the members of the Wholesalers Association named as complainants became hostile witnesses. At the pretrial examination, both denied ever making charges against Jacoby or anyone else. The pattern would continue throughout the trial.

For pretrial, defense argued that the industry war was a plot between Frank Martel, as Detroit Federation of Labor President, and Harry Rosman to ruin Jacoby's business. Jacoby had stood up to Martel and was Rosman's chief competitor. Judge Cotter responded by demanding an explanation for armed men at union meetings and Association dues to Abe Bernstein for protection.

The defense had no response; the men were held for trial.

The trial opened dramatically when Chief Assistant Prosecutor James Chenot explained to the court how the Purple Gang had systematically extorted money from Detroit area cleaners and dyers. He outlined the gang's method of extortion, painting a picture of the gang at its headquarters—the Jacoby cleaning plant—taking target practice and twirling pistols around their fingers.

The defense argued that the State's chief witness, Harry Rosman, and Labor President Frank X. Martel had extorted the unions and sold out the Retail Tailors to get a price increase for his racket. Abe Bernstein had been a reluctant arbitrator for the Wholesalers Association, and the Purple Gang a fiction created by Rosman and Martel.

But the Prosecution had checks. All of them had been signed by Harry Rosman and endorsed and cashed by Charles Jacoby.

Frank Martel complained to the Detroit press that the Purple Gang Trial was ignoring the crimes of the gang and turning into an indictment of his Detroit Federation of Labor. Martel would not testify as a witness, deeming it "a betrayal of the Detroit Federation of Labor."

On June 27th, 1928 the trial neared its end. Defense attorney Samuel Rhodes declared that when the State rested he would make a motion asking for a verdict of not guilty. Defense attorney Brown argued that his clients had not been effectively tied to a conspiracy and that their suspicious activities were "merely . . . isolated incident[s]." Defense also contended that the conflicting nature of the state's witnesses' testimony had cleared his clients.

On July 2nd, 1928 an unusual incident occurred. Samuel Rhodes asked Judge Bowles to reopen the case so that Charles Jacoby could be placed on the witness stand. Rhodes told the court that his client wanted to vindicate himself.

Jacoby blamed the terrorism on Frank Martel and labor leaders in the Detroit Federation of Labor. He maintained he hired Purple gangsters to succeed where the Detroit Police Department had failed, in protecting plants during a vicious industry war. He stated that labor leaders had gone so far as to attempt to poison a public food supply.

In its summation the State pleaded with the jury to consider the facts, emphasizing that the trouble in the Detroit cleaning and dyeing industry did not begin until the industry was organized by Chicago labor racketeers. Jacoby was the man who represented the association; he had been chosen as the only man with whom Chicago labor racketeers would do business; he had the Purple Gang force wholesalers to pay for protection, and when the money was forthcoming the pillaging ceased. The biggest threat to society was that the gang had used the Cleaners and Dyers war to infiltrate legitimate business by exploiting the gangster/businessman relationship between Abe Bernstein and brother-in-law Jacoby.

Defense attorneys Rhodes and Kennedy argued that rather than conspirators, Jacoby and gang were actually victims of the Cleaners and Dyers War. They characterized Frank Martel as "a ruler of stench bombers, window breakers and perjurers" declaring that the trail of corruption "leads directly to the door of the labor temple!"

On September 13th, 1928, the case was given to the jury. At the trial's inception, conviction had seemed certain but the defense had made a dent in the state's armor. The jurors were out little more than one hour before bringing in a verdict of not guilty.

Fear had colored the testimony of state witnesses. Following the acquittal Frank Martel was brought up on charges of extortion based on testimony given during the Purple Gang trial. Martel stood mute, a plea of not guilty was entered on his behalf, and he too was acquitted.

Estimates of tribute paid and damages incurred by shop owners during the Cleaners and Dyers War vary considerably. One cleaning plant owner claimed that certain Detroit labor leaders were getting as much as $200,000 dollars a year in graft from the industry. Detroit police records on reported property losses through 1928 totaled $161,000. This did not include cases that went unreported.

The Purple Gang trial did have one positive outcome. It ended the Cleaners and Dyers War. The Purple Gang, however, came through unscathed and lived to fight another day.

Chapter 7

The St. Valentine's Day Massacre

"The Purple Gang was a hard lot of guys, so tough they made Capone's playmates look like a Kindergarten class . . . Detroit's snooty set used to feel it was really living to talk to them hoodlums without getting their ounce brains blown out."

—Milton "Mezz" Mezzrow

"I will give you 24 hours to kill at least three and no more than six or else bring them in here. We don't care if you kill them off. The best crook is a dead crook!"

—Detroit Police Commissioner William P. Rutledge

On February 14th, 1929 a siren-filled black Cadillac carrying five men pulled to a stop in front of the S.M.C. Cartage Company in Chicago. Two police officers and two men in overcoats climbed out and walked briskly into the Cartage Company garage carrying riot-length shotguns.

The fifth man remained behind the wheel. In the back of the unheated garage, six well-dressed gangsters huddled around a coffee pot. A man in grease stained overalls worked on one of the trucks. A German Shepherd tied to a bumper barked as the patrolmen burst through the door.

The gangsters were ordered to face the wall. The men, members of the George "Bugs" Moran Northside Gang, grudingly complied, assuming a routine police shakedown. Either someone hadn't been paid off at the station or the raid was for good police publicity. They might even be honest cops who didn't know any better.

After confiscating their weapons, the uniformed men took several backward paces. In a flash of metal the detectives pulled Thompson submachine guns from their overcoats and took positions on either side of their prey. In an instant, all four men opened fire, spraying their victims' heads, backs and legs. Six gangsters were dead before their bodies hit the floor, falling straight back from where they stood.

The trench-coated killers then handed their smoking weapons to the uniformed men, raised their hands above their heads, and left the garage at gunpoint, "escorted" by the officers. They got into the waiting police car and tore off, siren screaming. Witnesses thought they'd seen a police raid—a common sight in Prohibition-era Chicago.

It was the howling of the dog that drew attention. Those who had the nerve to peek inside found the aftermath of the worst gangland slaughter in U.S. history. Its victims were identified as brothers Pete and Frank Gusenberg, the main enforcers of the Moran Gang; Albert Kashelleck (supposedly Moran's brother-in-law);

accountant and business manager, Adam Heyer; safe-cracking mechanic, John May; racketeer Albert Weinshank; and Dr. Reinhart H. Schwimmer, an optometrist and sometime bootlegger.

These men represented the heart of Chicago's once powerful Northside Mob. They'd been waiting that morning for Moran to join them. When the police arrived Frank Gusenberg was still barely alive.

He had more than 22 bullet wounds in his body. When asked who shot him, Gusenberg whispered, "No one—nobody shot me." He died in a hospital three hours later.

The S.M.C. Garage had been the liquor distributing center for the Northside Gang. Its members had gathered that cold St. Valentine's morning awaiting a large shipment of whiskey. It had been offered to Moran by an anonymous source for a bargain price.

The load was scheduled for 10:30 A.M., but the mobster was late to the rendezvous that morning. Moran had missed death by only minutes. As he and two gunmen walked to the garage they'd seen the siren-fitted Cadillac pull up and stayed away.

The killing was as clever as it was well-planned. It was as though members of the Chicago police force had actually been responsible for the massacre. It was soon discovered that the murders had been pulled off by five gangland assassins, two masquerading as police.

However, spotters had mistaken one of the men in the garage for "Bugs" Moran. The target was still alive. The killers had failed.

The massacre captured the public's imaginations, the brazen public slaughter enraged citizens. An investigation was immediately launched by the Chicago P.D. in conjunction with the State Attorney General's office as agents promised to move heaven and earth to apprehend the killers and clean up Chicago.

Across the street from the garage were two rooming houses. They had housed some very interesting young tenants. Mrs. Michael Doody, who owned one, told police that approximately ten days before the massacre two young men wanted rooms.

Mrs. Frank Orvidson, who ran the other boarding house, rented a room to a third man the same day. All three said they were cab drivers who worked nights. They insisted on rooms that faced the front of the building.

On the morning of the massacre these men mysteriously vanished. The Purple Gang was already suspected in the massacre. When the landladies were shown photographs of sixteen Purples, they identified Harry and Phil Keywell, and Eddie Fletcher. Both landladies stated that when they entered the men's rooms to clean them they would often find one or the other seated by the window.

The police speculated that the three had been used as spotters for the assassination team, a strategy typical of the Capone mob. Incredibly, the Detroit police never arrested them for questioning. Detroit Inspector Henry Garvin stated to the press that he didn't believe the Purple Gang could be involved in something this ruthless.

This was said in the aftermath of the Milaflores Massacre. Garvin's obstruction of justice not only revealed his corruption but allowed the gang to continue on their invincible violent path. The Purple Gang is suspected of having beaten the rap in hundreds of unsolved gangland murders probably due to such extensive political ties.

There are two theories for the reason behind the St. Valentine's Day Massacre. The first involved Capone. For more than a year prior to the killings, Al Capone had a loose business relationship with the Detroit mob, as the Purples distributed quality Canadian whiskey called Old Log Cabin.

Capone had always had a shaky relationship with Moran's gang, but gave him a deal to sell Purple Gang supplied whiskey in his part of town. Moran didn't like the price he was paying for it. When offered a cheaper supply by another hijacking outfit, Moran decided to terminate his arrangement with Capone, vis-à-vis the Purple Gang.

He peddled the cheap booze for the same price as Old Log Cabin while pocketing the difference. But customer's began to complain about the quality of the new whiskey. Moran was forced to go to Capone to beg for his consignment back, whereupon Capone cheerfully told Moran that it was already spoken for— he had been selling off Moran's supply.

Moran decided to solve his supply problem by hijacking whatever Old Log Cabin he needed. The Purple gang shipments were hijacked constantly. When Old Log Cabin began turning up at Moran-supplied Chicago speakeasies Capone and the Purples knew they needed a plan.

An agent gained Moran's trust by selling him cheap loads of "hijacked" Old Log Cabin from Purple Gang shipments. The day before the St. Valentine's Day Massacre, the agent baited Moran with a large shipment. Moran agreed to pick up the whiskey personally at the Garage. According to one account, it was Purple Gang boss Abe Bernstein who placed the fatal call.

The second theory is that the massacre was all about revenge. Moran sent men to kill one of Capone's principal lieutenants, "Machine Gun" Jack McGurn. For years the Northside gang had been trying to kill Capone, and eliminating this top enforcer might make it easier.

The Gusenberg brothers caught McGurn in a phone booth and blasted away. Leaving him for dead, they hurried back to Moran with the good news. Unfortunately for them, McGurn lived.

He also knew the Gusenbergs represented Bugs' Northside Gang. When he recovered, he went to Capone to get permission to eliminate the Northsiders once and for all. With Capone's blessing, McGurn planned the massacre.

A hit team was assembled that consisted of Fred Burke; James Ray, another Egan's Rats gunman; Joseph Lolardo; and two of the Capone organization's top killers, John Scalise and Albert Anselmi. Burke and Ray were to wear police uniforms so they wouldn't be recognized by Moran's boys.

These gangsters had walked in each other's territories for years but now they'd come together for one of the most sensational killings in organized crime's history. The first and only clue to the identities of the killers was the result of a traffic accident in Michigan at the end of the same year.

On the evening of December 14th, 1929 Forrest Kool was driving south on U.S. 12, headed for St. Joseph, Michigan, when a Hudson coupe heading in the opposite direction veered into his lane. Kool swerved hard to avoid a collision, but the Hudson coupe struck him and drove on.

Another driver who'd witnessed the accident followed the Hudson with Kool on the running board. Just up the road the men spotted it on the shoulder. Kool might've kept on going that night had he realized the driver of the coupe was Egan Rats' gunman Fred "Killer" Burke.

Burke had recently bought a hideout in the area, and he and his girlfriend had been there for several months. He was already wanted for robbery and murder. Most of the law enforcement agencies in the Midwest were looking for him.

When the men approached him, they noticed that he was drunk. He agreed to go look at the damage he'd done to Kool's car. He offered twenty-five dollars for the damages, but said he did not have anything smaller than hundreds. Kool wanted to call the police.

Burke replied, "Well, if that's what you want it suits me!" He actually helped straighten out the fender and then got back in his car. When he pulled onto the road, Kool followed him.

Just down the road, Burke pulled off again and waved Kool around him, then followed behind. As they arrived in St. Joseph Burke began blowing his horn as if to get Kool's attention. Hoping Burke had decided to settle for damages he pulled over, but this time Burke fled.

As Kool was describing the accident to an officer, the gangster drove by. The officer jumped on the running board of Kool's vehicle and ran down to Burke's car at a stop light. He leaped onto the running board and rode for several blocks until Burke stopped at a light, waited for it to turn green, and shot him at point blank range.

The officer collapsed in the street while Burke's car roared away. Burke wrecked the coupe further down the road and left the car. Police found his driver's license inside.

A raid of his hideout produced an arsenal of weapons: two machine guns, two automatic rifles, a sawed-off shotgun, several revolvers, and several hundred rounds of ammunition. Inside a bedroom closet was a valise containing $310,000 in stolen negotiable securities. Burke, meanwhile, had disappeared.

Headlines screamed Burke's Detroit underworld background and his role in the Milaflores Apartment Massacre in March of 1927. His membership in Joseph "Red" O'Riordan's Irish gang of violent kidnappers had made him famous years earlier, now he was suspected of the St. Valentine's Day Massacre.

The new science of ballistics had just gained credence by the time of the massacre. Major Calvin Goddard had proven that every firearm leaves a distinctive series of marks on the bullet as it passes through the barrel. No two weapons mark ammunition in the same pattern.

Each Valentine killer had provided a set of uniquely different mechanical fingerprints. The machine guns in Burke's hideaway were sent to Goddard's Chicago laboratory where he compared the bullets and shells to those collected at the scene of the massacre. The scientist concluded that bullets fired from one of the guns matched markings in the bodies of the victims.

On March 4th, 1929 the Chicago Police Department publicly named the participants in the St. Valentine's Day Massacre as Burke, James Ray, and Joseph Lolardo: Jack McGurn's assembled team of hitmen.

After receiving a life sentence, Burke arrived at Marquette Prison on April 28th, 1931 where he remained a model prisoner until his death from a heart attack in

1940. The Detroit police never arrested the Purples for their role in the massacre. Their cooperation with Capone was completely ignored.

By the late twenties the Purple Gang had reached the zenith of its power. They were asked to attend the first national underworld conference initiated by the notorious New York mob. This meeting of gang bosses from major cities of the U.S. which took place in Atlantic City, was rumored to have been organized by Charles "Lucky" Luciano, Meyer Lansky, and Johnny Torrio, rising stars in the New York underworld.

Torrio was a semi-retired boss who'd passed the mantle of leadership in Chicago on to Al Capone. At the conference were Capone and his business manager Jake "Greasy Thumb" Guzik, as well as bosses representing Boston, Philadelphia, Cleveland, Kansas City, and Detroit.

The purpose of the conference was to put an end to unnecessary violence escalating in the underworld over territorial disputes, hijacking and bidding for liquor shipments. The frequency of murders on crowded city streets had ignited public outcry for police action. Irate citizens forced authorities' hands, which resulted in loss of revenue for organized crime.

The conference was the birth of organized crime. A national federation of underworld gangs was formed whose leaders would meet to settle disputes between mobs. Each group was allowed to operate as it saw fit within its territory without interference from other gangs.

Their plan was to gain a national monopoly on the liquor trade. Proceeds from their prohibition profits would be put into distilleries and breweries should liquor become legal. The first national wire service was even established as a result of this conference.

For their contribution to the cause, the Purple Gang was extremely good at persuading recalcitrant blind pig operators into stocking the liquor and beer they sold. Even if the product was poor the incentive to buy it was good, as the mobsters kept their arguments in their shoulder holsters. Born in protection and hijacking rackets the Purples' talents extended to smuggling and transporting whiskey themselves.

The Purple Gang began taking over and buying into blind pigs and cabarets all over Detroit. Several Purple gangsters could merely walk into a blind pig and demand a cut of the day's profits. If they were crossed, the place would be shot up.

By 1929 they either controlled or had a cut of most of the Detroit area blind pig industry. Having conquered independent business, the gang took control of the many docks and boat slips along the Detroit riverfront. A cut was demanded from the profits of Canadian whiskey brought into port.

Rumrunners who failed to pay, lost their cargoes and their lives. Tribute was paid in cases of whiskey. Dealing with liquor meant dealing with the mob, and the mob was all about tribute for the right to operate.

Businessmen through and through, the gang developed a system by which they made 150% profit on every freely acquired bottle. The Purple Gang's distributors told blind pigs that they would sell them the whiskey at cost. Because they were selling the whiskey at cost, the distributor would explain, they required a share of the blind pig's profits, neglecting to mention that the whiskey had been acquired free for protection or hijacked from the pier.

Distributing whiskey this way was business genius because it gave the Purples financial leverage over the clubs. They gained controlling interest in many of the city's best cabarets and blind pigs. Not only were they taking a cut, but the whiskey was being cut and sold locally or shipped to the New York and Chicago mobs.

Cutting whiskey produced two and a half bottles for every one purchased or hijacked. The whiskey cutting process involved diluting the actual product with water and artificial flavoring then rebottling it. Bogus labels and tax stamps were affixed to the new bottles so they looked like the genuine article.

By the late twenties illegal liquor profits exceeded $215,000,000 annually, second only to automobile manufacturing. The liquid gold flowing into Detroit began to attract the attention of Al Capone. He traveled to Detroit personally to investigate the possibilities of establishing a Chicago foothold there.

But at the conference Capone was rebuked by the gang, who insisted "That is our river!" Capone instead arranged for them to supply him Canadian whiskey. He shrewdly made the Purples his liquor agents rather than going to war with them.

How the Mighty Fall

The Purples may have wielded control over the famous Al Capone, but they were facing trouble with the law and within their own gang. In 1929, Mabel Wildebrandt, Attorney General of Prohibition Enforcement, issued a directive to destroy the Purple Gang. It was an enormous task, but the Federal government had allocated funds for fighting Prohibition and ignited interest in the rum-running taking place on the Detroit River.

Prohibition agents set their sights on the Purple Gang. "Knock offs" or federal confiscation of whiskey, became more frequent. Payoffs had only been made to local officials, so between March and May of 1929, the Purples lost more than $90,000 worth of liquor to Federal agents.

The crackdown increased tensions on the streets. On the morning of May 2nd, two customs officers parked by the river, acting on a tip that a large shipment was due at the 24th Street pier. The two officers approached just as the first of three rumrunners' boats landed and its occupants unloaded cases into trucks.

The first boat was tied to the pier while the others remained anchored in the river. The agents crept out of the patrol car, pistols drawn. As soon as the runners spotted the agents they opened fire and officers, outnumbered, retreated and called for reinforcements. The gangsters continued loading their trucks until two carloads of agents pulled up. As officers approached the dock a freight train cut them off, but they climbed between cars and started shooting. One hundred rounds were exchanged.

Still the gangsters escaped, by climbing back through the cars of the train and speeding off in the agents' cars. The anchored boats also raced away. In the end two trucks and 98 cases of whiskey were confiscated by the officers.

In a surprise move by Federal agents, twelve Purple gangsters were arrested in May after five months of surveillance by a combined force of police detectives and Federal Prohibition agents. The blanket warrant charged them with conspiracy to violate the U.S. Dry Laws. The defense attorney attempted a release the following day claiming that with "2,700 provisions in the U.S. Code," the blanket warrant was far too vague.

But the specific charges were kept quiet. The agents

were hoping to use the Jones Stalker Act, referred to as the Jones law, which did not penalize for possession of liquor but for the manufacture, transportation, importation or sale of intoxicants for beverage purposes. The goal was to get the Purple Gang suspects under these provisions for many reasons.

The Jones law did not differentiate between old and new offenses. Whether or not violaters had to answer for past crimes was up to the judge, and the rum-running was a felony for which an alien could be deported. It was squarely aimed at underworld liquor traffickers.

On May 24th a Federal Grand Jury returned indictments against four important Purples arrested in the raids. The Purple Gang was going to court.

The withheld information was revealed during the trial. Three Special Treasury Agents had tapped the Purple's telephone lines. They'd transcribed numerous conversations between the defendants and their customers. This trial was the first incident of wire tapping used as evidence instead of liquor, and the first time that Purple gangsters faced a Federal judge.

The Hart Novelty Company and the Max Gordon Realty Company was the alias for their business. Agent Gregory Frederick explained to the jury that the four men, with no liquor for sale at the address, carried on a massive import/export business in liquor and beer. Frederick's testimony was an attempt to prove in court that the companies were actually an illegal liquor distributor's base of operations.

Checks, papers, and account books had been seized in a raid and were entered as evidence to support the wiretap transcripts. As with Al Capone, the gangsters were not broken by conviction for their crimes but by their own business records. The agents raided the apartment without a warrant, however, based on what they heard over the wiretap. An Inspector had ordered the raid after the gang members' arrest.

The account books and delivery receipts documented imports of liquor from Canada. Deliveries were made on the same day that telephone conversations relating to them were heard. If they were inadmissable, the case would be lost. The evidence could be used in Federal court only if the raid had been made without the advice or aid of the Feds who'd tapped the phones.

Inspector Patrick O'Grady was called by the defense. They attempted to draw an admission from O'Grady that he had consulted with Federal agents before ordering the raid on the Purple Gang's liquor distributing business. O'Grady proved the raid was legitimate by insisting that he'd instructed his men to pick up Purple gangsters "wherever they found them."

On July 24th, 1929, the Purple Gang defendants were found guilty of conspiracy to violate Prohibition. The jury was out only fifteen minutes before bringing in a guilty verdict. The four men were only sentenced to 22 months and fined $5000 each, but it was the first real blow by law enforcement agencies against the leadership of the Purple Gang. Even as the police attempted to destroy the Purples, the gang was so cutthroat that it was destroying itself—the powerful gang had begun to implode.

The Decline of the Purple Gang

Irving Shapiro was the first to go. Shortly after 3:00 A.M., on July 27th, 1929, residents were awakened by the sound of gunshots reverberating through their usually quiet neighborhood. Witnesses caught a glimpse of a speeding touring car. In the dim light one woman could make out the crumpled body of a man in the gutter.

Detectives quickly identified the body as that of Irving Shapiro, Purple Gang gunman and hijacker. A fifty dollar bill and an expensive watch were all that was found in Shapiro's pockets. All of the labels in his expensive suit had been cut off.

A private guard in the neighborhood had reported the large gray car that raced from the scene. By the time police arrived they found two .32 caliber slugs next to a crumpled body. The Wayne County Coroner confirmed their suspicions that Shapiro had been "taken for a ride."

He was shot from the back seat and his body shoved out of the car. He had been killed instantly. A bullet had entered the back of his head and exited under his right eye.

Irving Shapiro was only twenty-five, but his death was considered long overdue. Known in the underworld as "Little Irving," he was one of the toughest members of the gang, especially feared by police. Once he'd gotten into a dispute with another prisoner which ended when Shapiro put the man's eye out.

Irv had grown up on Detroit's Lower East Side with the original Purple gangsters. Always a tough guy, Shapiro was thrown out of Elementary School and later the Bishop ungraded school—spawning ground of the Purples. Although physically small, Shapiro always compensated for his size with savage behavior.

As an adult Shapiro was one of the Purple mob's most successful strong arm men ever to put the muscle on Detroit's blind pigs. He extracted thousands in protection money and strutted around town in expensive tailor made suits and late model luxury cars. A suspect in scores of Detroit gangland murders, he was never convicted of a serious crime.

By the time of his murder, Shapiro had been picked up more than twenty-four times for felonious assault, robbery, extortion, kidnapping, and murder. He had many enemies in the underworld and there were endless theories behind his execution. He expected blind pig operators to pay a 50 percent tribute to operate unmolested and was rumored to be reviving the big industry protection racket and its high profile kidnappings.

Shapiro muscled in on building trades through his control of the plumbers union, extorting more than $8,000 a month for protection. The gang set prices and dictated which plumbers would work on which contracts. It was so well organized that the extorted businesses were divided into districts with Purple gangsters as zone captains to insure no one escaped paying tribute to the gang.

When a police inspector began an investigation into the construction racket his home was bombed. Police believed that men from Max Ruben, head of the Motion Picture Operators Union, to Sam Gross, a wealthy racketeer, were successfully kidnapped and ransomed by the gang. Their terrorism knew no limits, even those of the legitimate business world.

They'd been running the well organized extortion racket for years and performing kidnappings on the side. On an anonymous tip, police picked up Purple associates who had been working with Shapiro kidnapping local businessmen. The tip confirmed their theory.

A $25,000 ransom sought by Shapiro's gang for a kidnapped contractor was argued down to only $4000.

Shapiro believed that he had been cheated by his partners when they split up $4000 instead of $25,000, and told Sam Bernstein and several other Purples that he was going to get his cut of the ransom or somebody was going to get hurt. That night he was murdered.

His car turned up in a used car lot three days after the shooting. Shapiro was the first Purple gangster ever to be taken for a ride. No one was brought to trial for his murder.

Shapiro's killing was only the beginning.

On October 28th, 1929, notorious Purple Gang gunman Zigmund "Ziggie" Selbin was shot to death while he cowered in a doorway on the city's West Side. Selbin had been caught on the street without his gun. A woman described to Detroit police how the gunman stood in the doorway where Selbin cowered and casually emptied his revolver into the Purple gangster.

The killer then walked away without looking back. A crowd gathered around the dying thug as he lay in a pool of his own blood. "Ziggie" Selbin was twenty-two years old.

Like his close friend, Irv Shapiro, the killing was long overdue. From the beginning of his career as a Purple gunman, Selbin had been a loose cannon.

Ziggie's police record showed nine arrests and no convictions. Most had been on serious charges. His specialty was extorting money from local merchants and hijacking blind pigs and other underworld havens.

Selbin was known as a mean drunk. During a binge in a blind pig he took a liking to a patron's ring. He asked for it, was promptly refused, then beat the man unconscious and tried without success to pull the ring off his finger. He then pulled a knife out of his pocket and removed the piece of jewelry, finger and all.

Ziggie made a habit out of holding up nightclubs and blind pigs belonging to the Hamtramck mob. The gang bought a lot of whiskey from the Purple Gang, and Selbin had been warned several times by Purple mob leadership to lay off. Finally, the Purple Gang and the Hamtramck mob had to make peace by agreeing on Ziggie Selbin's extermination.

Having threatened their security, Selbin was killed by his own gang. The last days of the roaring twenties were taking their toll on the manpower of the Purple Gang. Freelancing posed a threat to their leadership.

Besides receiving the first criminal convictions since their meteoric rise to power, the mob was finding itself having to take its own members for a ride. Gone, too were the days when they could kill authority figures like Polakoff or Vivian Welch in cold blood. The next major gangland incident exposed the police that had protected them.

❖❖❖

Inspector Henry J. Garvin was the department's self-proclaimed Detroit underworld nemesis. On January 2nd, 1930, he pulled out of his driveway and turned his patrol car toward headquarters. He drove slowly that early winter morning and did not notice the black sedan pull up shortly after he left home.

Garvin heard a horn behind him and pulled over to let the car pass. As the Model A pulled up Garvin noticed curtains drawn across the back windows, but it was too late to act. Two gunmen armed with a .45 pistol and a shotgun opened fire.

One of the first rounds grazed the back of the police officer's head. As he slumped to the floor, the gunmen poured round after round into his car, which rolled up over the curb and stalled in a snowdrift. Assuming

Garvin to be dead, the gunmen raced away.

Dazed and bleeding, Garvin crawled out of the battered car. He had received only superficial wounds, avoiding the fire by falling to the floor. As he rolled out into the snow he could hear a child whimpering, a little girl who had been walking to school had been caught by a bullet. Her injury would bring public scrutiny upon his attack.

Police officials theorized that Garvin had been targeted because of the pressure his Crime and Bomb Squad was exerting on organized crime. But in the underworld, rumor tells the real story. It had been said that the inspector failed to keep promises he made to gang leaders in exchange for information, but his very necessary execution was botched and now everyone was exposed.

In January of 1930, a Board of Inquiry was assembled to investigate shattering allegations made by Detective Van Coppenolle, a member of the Black Hand Squad. Two months prior to Garvin's attack, Van Coppenolle had claimed to have accompanied the chief of the Black Hand Squad to a meeting with Italian gunmen where Garvin's murder was arranged.

When the shooting took place, Van Coppenolle was dragged before the Police Trial Board to tell what he knew about the incident. By that time he'd told police officials several different stories, and was charged with "conduct unbecoming an officer." His allegations, however, initiated a full departmental investigation.

Van Coppenolle's story was that he attended a meeting with gangsters at the Book-Cadillac Hotel and was informed Garvin would die for double crossing members of the Laman mob, who'd paid $20,000 to insure that their hired kidnapper would only be tried for extortion. Garvin had gotten him out of prison on an extortion charge only to have the gunman stand trial in another kidnapping case. He was convicted and given fifty years.

Van Coppenolle's account was supported by the detective's partner, who claimed that he had waited inside the door of the hotel suite but did not actually attend the meeting. They explained their presence at the meeting by claiming to have been negotiating a kidnap victim's release, but that they were too late and the victim was already dead. When the victim's body was found Van Coppenolle's claim was further validated.

The gangster to whom Van Coppenolle attributed the statements was called before the Police Trial Board. He took the Fifth. The gangster's refusal to deny meeting with Van Coppenolle really made the story stick.

Trial board testimony also revealed Garvin's exploits to have been protected on high, as far up as the mayor. But the most damaging report came from Detectives William Delisle and Roy Pendergrass. They worked for Garvin in the Crime and Bomb Squad and had quite a story to tell.

The detectives saw five Purple gangsters come out of the Addison Hotel and climb into a Cadillac sedan. Delisle recognized one of the Bernstein brothers and decided to question the men, as it was at the height of the Cleaners and Dyers War.

As the detectives approached, Delisle saw Ray Bernstein shove a pistol under the seat. Startled, both officers pulled their guns and ordered the men out of the car. All armed, the five were arrested and booked.

Delisle and Pendergrass were thrilled. Four were caught with weapons, and Ray Bernstein was seen throwing his gun under the seat. It looked as though the detectives had finally arrested the most powerful Purple Gang leaders on a charge that might stick. The Cadillac was traced to Charles Jacoby, brother-in-law of the Bernstein brothers and Cleaners and Dyers War magnate.

Inspector Garvin called Detective Delisle at home after he got off of work—it was 2 A.M. He informed the detective that it was on the orders of the Mayor that no warrants be issued for these men. Delisle said that they were already planning to obtain a warrant on their report later that day.

Garvin waited until 5 A.M. to call Delisle's partner, Pendergrass, and repeated the mayor's orders. He explained that he'd already had a second report written stating the detectives found the guns on the ground rather than on the Purple gangsters. Later that day Garvin called Pendergrass in and ordered him to go to the prosecutor for an arrest warrant, basing the concealed weapons charge on the erroneous second report.

Pendergrass was refused the warrant and the Purples were released. But it was not over for the detectives. It actually got worse.

Delisle received a call from Chief of Detectives Fox, who wanted Delisle and Pendergrass to make a written statement explaining the discrepancies in the two reports. Fox had somehow gotten hold of their true reports, despite Garvin's promise that he'd destroyed them. Delisle and Pendergrass went to Garvin's home.

Again Garvin told the detectives that the release of the Purples was on the mayor's orders and it must stand. He agreed to clarify the discrepancies between their reports and his with the proviso that they never talk about the incident.

After this damaging testimony, the mayor appeared before the Police Board to disclaim allegations that he had the Purple gangsters released, calling the story a "black lie." Garvin avoided testifying at the Police Board trial based on Doctors' claims of illness. After the usual setbacks, three of the original five were re-arrested and Garvin was forced to tell his story during their pretrial examination.

He claimed he changed the reports because the detectives told him they'd found the guns on the ground. According to Garvin, "It was . . . not probable that the two officers should corral five men in an automobile and after ordering them out find pistols on all of them. Gangsters in such circumstances are usually quick to ditch pistols. I called the officers to congratulate them... providing the search and seizure had been properly made. They then admitted that the pistols were not on the men when found." The intimidated Delisle and Pendergrass did not dispute Garvin's testimony.

Defense attorney Kennedy argued that the detectives had no probable cause to stop and search the men as no felony had been committed. The Judge ruled that the arrest was based on an unreasonable search and seizure, and the Purples were released.

Although they escaped conviction, much had been exposed of the gang's police connections and operating procedures. The failed execution of Henry Garvin was an ominous sign of organized crime's new vulnerability. Previously untouchable, the Purple Gang was getting sloppy.

❖❖❖

Corrupt police and freelancing gang lieutenants were not the only destructive forces, with the gang's booming prosperity had come luxuries that by now started to divide them. In May of 1930, Joe Bernstein drove to the home of his close friend and business partner, Harry Kirschenbaum. Harry, ex-convict and Purple gangster, was an opium addict who'd promised to kick his narcotics habit once and for all.

Kirschenbaum's filling pad company was a good front for Joey Bernstein's end of the Purple Gang's lucrative wire service operation. It provided Detroit's 700 handbooks with indispensable daily horse racing information. Subscribing to the Purple Gang's wire service was not an option for handbook operators—those who went elsewhere or objected to paying for protection went out of business, permanently.

Bernstein depended on Kirschenbaum. He was one of the Purples' most capable lieutenants. Lately, however, Harry's use of opium had been creating serious problems.

The responsibility to oversee the Purple Gang's handbooks was a job which required daily monitoring, but Kirschenbaum would disappear for days at a time. Bernstein had begun to lose his famous hair trigger temper. He was known in the underworld for moodiness and for being the most physically dangerous Bernstein brother.

Several days earlier, Bernstein stopped by Kirschenbaum's home but was told by his wife that Harry was out. Joe noticed the pungent smell of opium in the house and suspected Kirschenbaum was back on the pipe. On this day he went to the house unarmed but had already decided that if he found Kirschenbaum smoking he would beat him within an inch of his life.

He burst into the house and asked where Harry was. Mrs. Kirschenbaum cried that her husband had been on a six week binge and was laying practically motionless in an upstairs bedroom.

"I'll take care of that baby!" Joe yelled as he pulled off his coat, and bounded up the stairs. He lunged at Kirschenbaum, who, anticipating the brutal beating, promptly pulled a pistol. Bernstein doubled back but Kirschenbaum shot him. The bullet tore through Bernstein's spleen as he stumbled down the steps and crashed through a locked door into the street.

Kirschenbaum then continued after Bernstein, firing as he ran. Joe staggered up Courtland Avenue and finally collapsed in front of a grocery store. Assuming that Joe Bernstein was dead, Kirschenbaum tossed the Mauser pistol into some bushes and ran back to his home for another pistol before racing off in his car.

A construction worker named George Barrett heard the commotion and saw Kirschenbaum throw away his pistol. He picked up the gun and fired at Kirschenbaum, who returned fire as he roared away in his car. Bernstein was rushed to the hospital with little hope for survival.

These were fellow gang members, who'd survived the street and gotten rich. Now they were turning on each other like common thugs. In view of their pasts, their lack of conscience was not surprising. But during the strong years of the Purple gang, partners would never have sunk to this and it was rather a pathetic ending to their long careers.

❖❖❖

Joe Bernstein had come a long way in thirty years. Right before the shooting he had built a Tudor style mansion in an exclusive neighborhood. He appeared in public as a prosperous businessman. He wintered in Florida, drove luxury automobiles, and seemed to have unlimited amounts of money.

Unlike legitimate businessmen, Joey Bernstein was

chauffeured by a bodyguard in a custom built Cadillac limousine. The luxury sedan was really an armored car. Its inside was lined with bulletproof steel and the windows were made of bulletproof glass.

Police Department records and underworld rumor painted the true picture of the suave thug. He'd been arrested fifteen times in ten years, but was convicted only once. He pled guilty and was given probation because of his youth. Other arrests included assault, extortion, gambling, and murder.

By the time Joe was in his late twenties, he had become a Purple mob boss, respected and feared. He had muscled the Detroit handbook operators into line and started the first wire service. The Purple Gang provided the bookmakers with race results, odds, scratch sheets, and betting information, maintaining an iron grip on gambling with control of the race wire.

Throughout the twenties, Bernstein maintained legitimate business fronts from barber shops to clothing stores to auto parts companies. These incomes supplemented his gangster earnings.

His partner Harry Kirschenbaum came to Detroit in 1924 from New York City. Kirschenbaum was first arrested for burglary at the age of sixteen. In 14 years he was arrested eighteen times, with four convictions.

He had served terms in Elmira Reformatory and Sing Sing before arriving in Detroit, and his three New York felony convictions made him eligible for sentencing under the state's Baume Law statutes; a fourth felony in New York could get Kirschenbaum a life sentence as an habitual criminal. This probably helped motivate his move to Detroit.

His underworld experience in betting made him an invaluable aid to Joe Bernstein, but his addiction ruined him. Upon searching Kirschenbaum's home after his assault on Bernstein, police found a large store of narcotics worth several thousand dollars, a number of shotguns and pistols, and a still hot opium pipe.

After two blood transfusions, Bernstein, still dangerously weak, was questioned by Detective Lt. William Johnson.

"How do you feel, Joe?" Johnson asked.

"Why, I am feeling fine," whispered Bernstein.

"Able to talk about the shooting?"

"You know I am not going to talk about anything."

In true underworld fashion Bernstein remained closemouthed. The refusal to file a complaint against Kirschenbaum would have let him remain free, but George Barrett, the construction worker who'd tried to stop Kirschenbaum, had been shot in the abdomen while chasing him.

Harry Kirschenbaum was arrested in Los Angeles and sent back to stand trial for assault with intent to kill George Barrett. Subpoena'd, Bernstein continued to protect his partner, and lied to the court that on the day of the shooting Kirschenbaum asked him to come to his house. Bernstein claimed that he thought the couple were having a domestic squabble, stating "I had straightened them out once before."

Bernstein said he walked into the room and was hit on the head. That was the last thing he remembered. When a lieutenant had told him that Kirschenbaum shot him, he couldn't believe it because he and Harry Kirschenbaum were good friends.

Harry Kirschenbaum was found not guilty, but was later convicted for violation of the Harrison Narcotics Act and sentenced to Federal prison. George Barrett sued Joe Bernstein in civil court for his medical bills.

Both Abe and Joe Bernstein promised to take care of them.

The suit was settled out of court.

As a result of the shooting, Joe Bernstein began to distance himself from the day-to-day operations of the Purple Gang to become a legitimate businessman. Businesses that operate to this day could have been founded in such a manner. Organized crime had succeeded in penetrating the business world.

The summer of 1930 marked the beginning of significant changes in Detroit society. The Purple Gang suffered the first successful conviction of leaders in a murder case. It seemed that an organization too wild to be civilized by society, was not able to survive itself.

The city also witnessed the beginning of the Great Depression and all of its devastation. No jobs and no money meant the city was ruled by the only power left, that of organized crime.

Chapter 8

Bloody July

"We have eleven murders in twelve days—speaking of crime—and Mr. Bowles says, 'Scientists employ parasitestodestroyoneanother.MaybethisisanactofProvidence in the killings of these gangsters.' Bullets are not distinctive. Neither is the law when It comes to defining the occupations of those who shall be accused of murder."

—Gerald Buckley,
Radio Commentator, July 21, 1930

1930 would prove to be an eventful year for Detroit as well as for the nation. Charles Bowles took office as a new mayor in an administration that would end in recall within six months. For the first time a Purple gangster would be convicted of murder.

The manufacturing centers of the midwestern U.S. were feeling the effects of the stock market crash. As demand for production decreased, industrial workers found themselves without a job.

The City of Detroit was paying out almost two million dollars a month to the growing army of the unemployed. The media reported that the worst was over, while the working class feared the future. The city was in the midst of the worst crime wave in its history.

The Fish Market Murders of 1930, in which representatives of the Eastside and Westside mobs were brutally slain, started a major underworld war that moved out into the streets. Shoot-outs between rival gunmen caught residents in the crossfire. Between May 31st and July 23rd, more than fourteen men died.

At least eleven were murdered in the first twelve days of the month. The local newspapers began referring to the carnage as "Bloody July."

While the Mafia war raged, the Purple Gang was tightening control over the brewing business.

The Purples now controlled most of the plants in the city, as cutting genuine whiskey proved much cheaper than producing bootleg hooch. By 1928, 150 large scale cutting plants were estimated to be operating in Detroit. Many ran twenty-four hours a day to supply large and constant demand.

Once the operation was perfected, one case could be turned into three or four cases of cut product. By the late twenties the Prohibition Director of Minnesota declared that out of 350,000 gallons of rye, bourbon, and scotch confiscated by his agents over a two year period, less than three gallons were genuine. With half the city out of work, the watered down whiskey probably tasted just fine.

The cutting process was simple chemistry. Pure whiskey was poured into vats and hot water added. After cooling down, alcohol was added to boost the proof to between 85 and 100. Caramel was then mixed in to give the liquid a whiskey color.

Oil of rye was often used for the flavor of real whiskey. As a finishing touch, a little fusel oil or glycerin was added to give the whiskey a "bead"—a thin layer of water on the surface of good whiskey. Many thought beading could only be acquired through aging.

The location of cutting plants was a carefully guarded secret to prevent hijacking, police shakedowns and federal raids. The accidental discovery of a Purple Gang cutting plant in July of 1930 resulted in the unnecessary killing of a seventeen-year-old black youth and the first successful murder prosecution of a Purple gangster.

Arthur Mixon was driving a horse-drawn wagon that hot July night in Detroit's Lower East Side, peddling ice off the back of the wagon with friends. Suddenly Mixon stopped. He climbed down from the wagon and peered underneath the doors of an old barn. According to one account, his ball had rolled under the barn doors. He had no idea that the building was a Purple Gang cutting plant. An associate of the gang noticed Mixon looking into the barn, and informed Phil Keywell.

In the meantime, Mixon and his friends got back into the wagon and drove to the corner of Hendrie and Hastings Streets. Mixon went into a bakery while the others waited outside. While Mixon was inside, six Purples approached the kids and demanded to know what business they had at the barn.

An argument ensued just as Mixon walked out. When the Purples asked Mixon what he was doing, he replied with a sarcastic remark. An accompanying gangster turned to Phil Keywell and said, "Put him on the spot."

Keywell pulled a revolver and shot Mixon. The youngster staggered for about twenty-five feet before collapsing in the street. The thugs ran back to the alley towards the cutting plant, but the police had surrounded the block.

Mixon was pronounced dead on arrival at the hospital. Officers had stopped Phil Keywell but released him when detectives ran up and called them away, claiming that a black man was responsible for the shooting. Keywell would later be identified by four witnesses as the man who killed Mixon.

Many years later another witness to the murder claimed that Mixon's life could have been saved; that the police ignored him while he bled to death, pausing to take depositions before calling an ambulance.

On September 20th, 1930, $2000 bail money was mysteriously provided for witnesses in protective custody at police headquarters. Both witnesses were friends of Arthur Mixon, who had positively identified Keywell. Wayne County Prosecutor Duncan C. McCrea begged that the youngsters be rearrested.

The bondsmen claimed they were acting on behalf of a sister of the boys. But when detectives checked their story, they found that the family knew nothing about bailing the youngsters out—under the circumstances, the family had preferred the safety of police custody. Police believed the Purple Gang had put up the bail in order to have the boys released so they could be murdered.

On September 23rd, Phil Keywell was picked out of a prisoner lineup by a friend of Mixon. The Arthur Mixon Murder Trial opened before Judge Thomas M. Cotter on October 6, 1930. Four neighborhood associates of Phil Keywell were sworn in as witnesses for the defense.

All defense witnesses were later charged with perjury, but only Josef Kassof, one of the boys walking by the scene of the murder, was ever tried. Kassof was found not guilty on a motion from the prosecutor.

The Mixon case was given to the jury on October 8th, 1930. After deliberating more than twenty-five hours, Judge Cotter dismissed the jury and reassigned the case. It's easy to see how organized crime could simply wear out the law to avoid conviction. But finally justice prevailed when a new jury came in with a first degree murder conviction after an hour and a half.

Philip Keywell had the distinction of being the first Purple ever convicted on a murder charge. He stood before Judge Thomas Cotter and was sentenced to life imprisonment. When asked by Cotter if he had anything to say, Keywell replied, "I am not guilty."

The Purple Gang's paper thin alibis were finally beginning to wear through. In the past, when police tried to get depositions from the victims of the holdup, most not only refused to admit that they were robbed but denied that a holdup had even taken place. Once Phil actually admitted his part in the heist but refused to name his accomplices and the only witness who agreed to testify wouldn't identify him.

Many witnesses to crimes would not testify against a reputed Purple gangster in the early twenties. But by 1930, despite an appeal, Philip Keywell's murder conviction was reviewed by the Michigan Supreme Court, and upheld. The unchecked criminal power of the twenties was beginning to unravel.

Organized Crime Out of Control

As crime intensified during the summer of 1930, mob killings began occuring in public with alarming frequency. Innocent bystanders were getting killed in the crossfire, and the citzens demanded answers. Two public killings at the LaSalle Hotel sparked a media witch hunt.

It started with the Bowles administration. Mayor Bowles had been a Judge before running for the mayoral office in 1929. When he became mayor he appointed attorney Harold Emmons Police Commissioner, and homicide squad inspector Patrick O'Grady Superintendent of Police. With these men, Bowles promised, the city would be cleaned up. But as murder rates increased many citizens came to view the Bowles administration as nothing more than a tool of the underworld.

To make matters worse, Mayor Bowles complained of being misquoted by the local press and issued orders to all subordinates to refuse interviews. Political observers theorized that it was this alienation of the press that led to his recall.

The city that distrusted its own mayor had spiraled out of control. The LaSalle Hotel was host to the fateful attacks that exemplified Detroit's blatant mob violence. It's difficult to imagine today that in 1930, one could sit in a hotel lobby and witness mob executions.

On July 3rd, three gangsters were sitting in a parked car outside the hotel engaged in casual conversation. As the last of rush hour traffic crawled towards home, a six foot, dark complexioned man in a Panama hat strode out of the hotel. He pulled a pistol out of his jacket and began firing into the open window of the car.

George Collins was in the passenger seat. The first bullet hit his chest at point blank range. The gunman methodically turned his pistol on the driver, William Cannon, who was frantically working at the steering wheel to maneuver out of the tight parking space. As he threw open the door to run, a slug tore through his neck and he collapsed into the street in a pool of his own blood.

The man in the back seat, Mike Stitzel, played dead but the ruse didn't work. The gunman turned his pistol on Stitzel's body and fired several rounds before casually replacing it in a shoulder holster and disappearing into the hotel crowd.

William Cannon and George Collins were minor Chicago gangsters who had been forced out of the city. They were known by Chicago police as small time heist artists and hijackers who attempted to muscle in on a beer syndicate that supplied the suburbs south of Chicago. The syndicate was affiliated with Capone, and the Capone mob had given the two thugs a choice: leave or die.

Two gold badges inscribed "Special Police" were found in the pockets of Cannon and Collins. Police figured the men were presenting themselves as law officers to speakeasies and then robbing them. Mike Stitzel had once been a doorman at a local gambling house and was probably a spotter for the two gunmen.

The men were no strangers to police. Cannon had a record of fifteen arrests in Detroit and Chicago, including impersonating an officer. George Collins had also been arrested fifteen times in Indiana, Illinois, and Michigan. Mike Stitzel was a small time Detroit gangster with twelve arrests on minor charges and no convictions.

Stitzel had survived, and admitted to detectives that he had known the pair for several years. They were using police badges to knock over speakeasies. Police believed that their hijacking of underworld operators was the reason for their murders and that Stitzel just happened to be at the wrong place at the wrong time.

It would be nearly a year before a Collins/Cannon murder indictment. The actual killer was identified as Leonard "Black Leo" Cellura. But Cellura had vanished.

On July 28, 1936, Leonard "Black Leo" Cellura casually walked into the Homicide Squad Room at Detroit police headquarters and turned himself in. He had been a fugitive for more than six years. Cellura admitted shooting Collins and Cannon to death but claimed self-defense.

Nicknamed "Black Leo" because of his dark complexion, Leonard Cellura was born in Italy in 1892, and immigrated to the U.S. with his family in 1908. Cellura was charged with the July 3rd murders of George Collins and William Cannon and stood mute while a plea of not guilty was entered on his behalf.

The State was not ready to proceed with a trial because of difficulties finding witnesses. His first courtroom appearance ended in a mistrial. Eventually he was convicted of first degree murder and sentenced to life.

But it was the next murder that would make Detroit shrink in astonishment and fear. Cellura's LaSalle roommate committed the most public slaying yet.

It was during the early summer of 1930 that the nightly tirades of Gerald E. Buckley against the Bowles administration and the local underworld created problems for both institutions. Buckley was an outspoken WMBC radio commentator who'd been born into money in a predominantly Irish section of Detroit nicknamed Corktown.

He had been educated in local parochial schools and eventually earned a law degree from the Detroit

Murder, Inc. hitman Harry "Happy" Maione. He was known as "Happy" because of the perpetual sneer on his face. (Municipal Archives of the City of New York)

Harry "Pittsburgh Phil" Strauss. Strauss died in the electric chair in New York's Sing Sing Prison. (Municipal Archives of the City of New York)

Sam Cohen (*left*) and Sam Kert. The "Two Sammies" distributed liquor for the Purple Gang. (Walter P. Reuther Library, Wayne State University)

Collingwood Massacre Trial, 1931. *Front row, l to r:* Wayne County Assistant Prosecutor Miles N. Culihan, Irving Milberg, Ray Bernstein, Harry Keywell, and Purple Gang attorney Edward Kennedy Jr. (Detroit News Archives)

Collingwood Massacre Trial, 1931. Harry Toy was the prosecutor (*far left, leaning back*). The Purple Gangsters were defended by Attorneys Edward Kennedy Jr. and Rodney Baxter (*right of table, front row*). Immediately behind Kennedy are the defendants, *l to r*, Harry Keywell, Irving Milberg, and Ray Bernstein. (Detroit News Archives)

Charlie Leiter, Oakland Sugar House Gang Boss and one of the Purple Gang's early mentors. (Courtesy of the David Lewis Family)

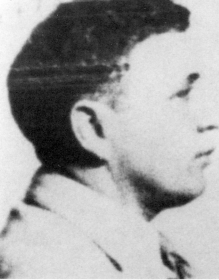

Henry Shorr. A leader of the
Oakland Sugar House Gang
and mentor of the Purples.
Shorr disappeared in Dec.
1934.
(Author's collection)

Zigmund "Ziggie" Selbin, Purple Gang gunman who once cut off a man's finger because he liked his ring. Selbin was shot to death in 1929 at age 22. (Burton Historical Collection, Detroit Public Library)

Harry Millman, Purple
Gang outlaw. Millman
relentlessly started trouble with the Italian mob
before being assassinated
by two Murder, Inc. hit-
men. (Burton Historical
Collection, Detroit Public
Library)

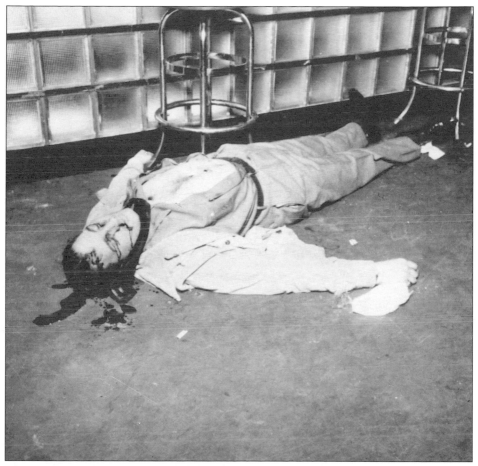

The bullet-riddled body of Harry Millman, shot to death before a crowd of horrified customers at Boesky's Restaurant in Detroit, on November 25th, 1937. (Author's collection)

The Graceland Ballroom in Lupton, Michigan, hideout of choice for mid-western gangsters on the lam in the mid-30s. It was built by Purple Gangster "One-Armed" Mike Gelfand. (Rose City Michigan Public Library)

The Old Bishop School on Winder Street, birthplace of the Purple Gang. (Detroit News Archives)

Joey Bernstein (*left*) and Purple Gang attorney Edward Kennedy Jr. (Walter P. Reuther Library, Wayne State University)

Philip Keywell, who in 1930 murdered a 17-year-old boy for peeking into a Purple Gang cutting plant. (Author's collection)

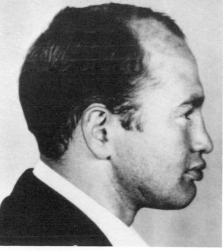

Sam "Gorilla" Davis, Purple
Gang enforcer.
(Author's collection)

Myron "Mike" Selik, key suspect
in the 1945 murder of State
Senator Warren Hooper. (Burton
Historical Collection, Detroit
Public Library)

Raymond Bernstein.
(Detroit Public Library)

Abe Axler (*seated*) and cronies (*standing left to right*) Philip
Keywell, Abe Zussman, and Willie Laks.
(Author's collection)

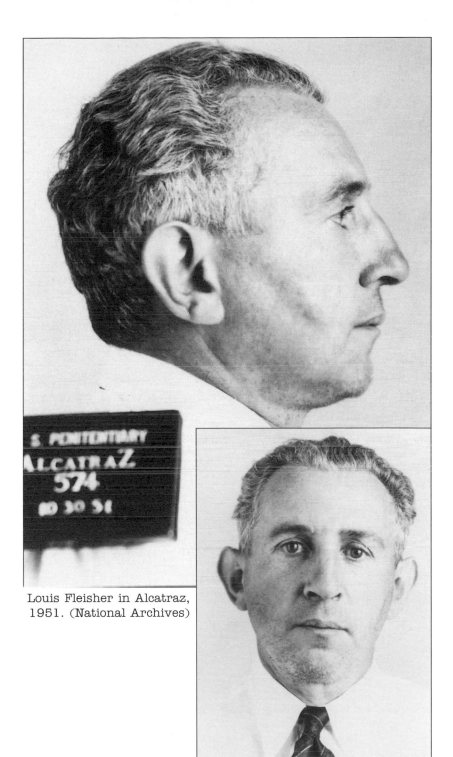

Louis Fleisher in Alcatraz,
1951. (National Archives)

Joey Bernstein at Detroit Police Headquarters during the
Ferguson Grand Jury investigation, Aug. 12, 1940. (Walter P.
Reuther Library, Wayne State University)

Abe Bernstein (*seated*) and his attorney during the Ferguson
Grand Jury investigation, 1940. (Burton Historical Collection,
Detroit Public Library)

This is what police found in Louis and Nellie Fleisher's Highland Park apartment. (Walter P. Reuther Library, Wayne State University)

Harry Fleisher, 1932. (Walter P. Reuther Library, Wayne State University)

The body of Isadore "Izzie the Rat" Sutker, among the casualties in the Collingwood Massacre, 1931. (Walter P. Reuther Library, Wayne State University)

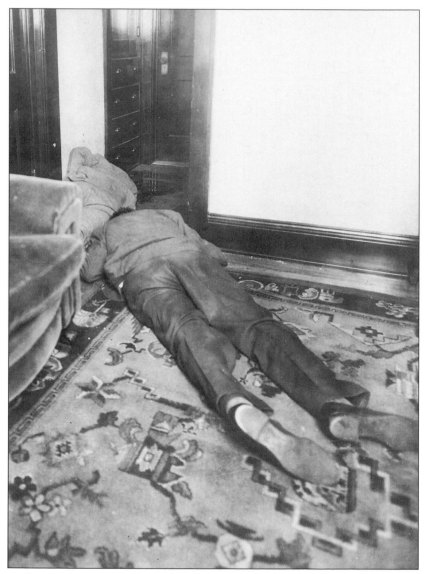

The bodies of "Nigger" Joe Lebovitz and Hymie Paul after the
Collingwood Massacre.

Aftermath of the Collingwood Massacre. Three dead bodies: Isadore Sutker, *left, near the bed;* Hymie Paul, *right foreground;* "Nigger" Joe Lebovitz, *center background.* (Walter P. Reuther Library, Wayne State University)

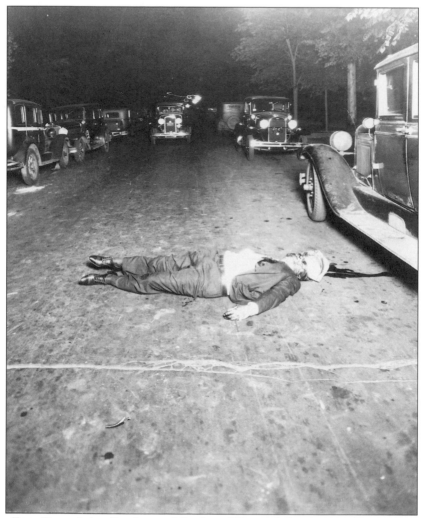

Ben Bronstein, freelance hijacker. His mistake: trying to steal a load of Purple Gang liquor.

Harry Millman's LaSalle Coupe after his enemies wired 10 sticks of dynamite to the spark plug. Millman missed out on the blast but his valet was blown to pieces. (Author's collection)

Raymond Bernstein (*far side of the table in front*) and Isadore Bernstein (*behind Raymond, next to the hat*) at a 1930 trial in which they and three other Purple Gangsters were charged with carrying concealed weapons. (Walter P. Reuther Library, Wayne State University)

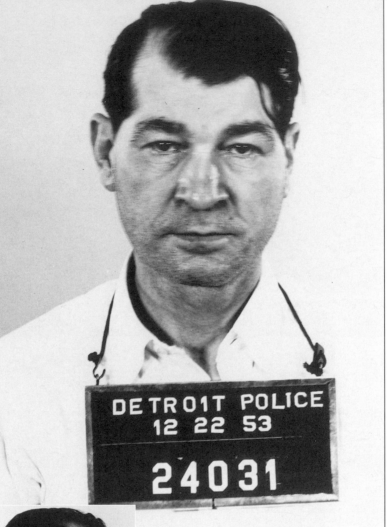

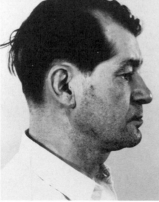

Abe Zussman, a.k.a. "Abie the Agent." Zussman was one of the most efficient Purple Gang killers. (Author's collection)

Eddie Fletcher, former prize-
fighter, who along with Abe
Axler terrorized the Detroit
underworld for eight years.
Fletcher and Axler were eventually murdered by their own
gang. (Author's collection)

Harry Fleisher (*second from left*), Charlie Leiter (*to Fleisher's right*), Henry Shorr (*to Leiter's right*), and other Oakland Sugar House Gangsters in a police photo, 1928. (Author's collection)

Purple Gangsters by the numbers: Irving Shapiro, one of the gang's most feared gunmen, #24151; Ziggie Selbin, #32548; Philip Keywell, #27946; Phil's younger brother Harry, #31279. (Author's collection)

Isadore Bernstein,
youngest of the four
Bernstein brothers and the
least criminally
talented. (Author's
collection)

Irving Milberg, famously accurate gunman and one of the
shooters in the Collingwood
murders. Milberg died in
prison. (Author's collection)

Harry Keywell, one of the
gunmen in the
Collingwood Massacre.
(Author's collection)

Meyer Cohen, better known as "Jew Max." His mistake: trying to double cross the Purple Gang in a 1932 whiskey deal. (Author's collection)

College of Law. He was also known as a womanizer and a nightclub patron. He once told several close friends that he decided to crusade against the local underworld as an investigator for Ford Motor Company. There he saw firsthand what the temptations of gambling and vice could do to poor working class families of industrial workers. Buckley broke into radio as a singer and eventually became a news commentator for WMBC. He used his radio show as a forum for attacks on corruption and organized crime.

From a radio studio in the LaSalle Hotel, Buckley had been speaking out against gambling and other rackets. As organized crime grew shamelessly public in the spring and summer 1930, the popular commentator targeted Mayor Bowles. On air, he accused the Detroit underworld and high ranking officials in the Bowles administration of collusion, of placing mobsters above the law.

Public clamor for the recall of Mayor Bowles had already begun with the dismissal of his Police Commissioner, Harold Emmons. The mayor had left town to see the Kentucky Derby and in his absence the Commissioner (egged on by the media) conducted police raids on handbook operations. Newspapers declared the raids a major blow against the underworld, although in reality they'd had little effect on local crime.

Before his trip, Bowles had asked Emmons for his resignation because he'd been unsuccessful in disciplining the police department and in coping with organized crime. Emmons had already been replaced with a former F.B.I. agent named Thomas Wilcox.

The newspapers claimed that Emmons's raids proved him to be incorruptible. They pointed to what a police commissioner could do when his hands were not tied by a corrupt mayor. To the public it appeared that Emmons was fired because he attacked the mayor's gambling interests in his absence.

Gerald Buckley hammered away at the Bowles administration during broadcasts but, curiously, did not support the recall movement, claiming it was undemocratic. The night before the vote, Buckley prepared a speech urging that the recall be defeated, and gave Bowles a copy before he went on the air. But on air Buckley reversed his position.

For weeks Buckley had been receiving daily death threats. His attacks on the Bowles administration had embarrassed the police and they in turn cracked down on the gangsters. Raids on underworld gambling resorts and the shutting down of rackets enraged local racketeers.

The Detroit gangsters kept growing stronger. Now they were so fearless that they planned the murder of a man who appeared on the radio every night, and expected no consequences. He was promised that if the recall election succeeded he would die. On the night of the election, Buckley took a cab from the City Hall to the LaSalle Hotel. He went into the studio where, at 12:15 A.M. he received a personal phone call from an unidentified woman. Buckley agreed to meet the woman in the hotel lobby.

At 1:30 A.M. he sat next to Jack Klein, a hotel resident, in LaSalle's lobby. That night, Buckley's wife received the final threat. The caller said simply, "Your husband won't be coming home tonight," and hung up.

At 1:45 A.M. three men strode into the hotel. They walked quickly and silently to where Buckley sat reading the newspaper and opened fire on the radio commentator right in the lobby. Klein had caught the gleam of a pistol and dove to the floor, but the gunfire was all directed at Buckley.

The three gunmen rushed out to a getaway car while a second car slid sideways and screeched to a stop blocking the Woodward Ave. entrance to Adelaide St., giving the gunmen a protected escape route. The driver—a woman—then abandoned the car and ran into the theater across from the hotel.

The woman, later identified as Lucille Love, was a girlfriend of local mobster Angelo Livecchi. She told police that she had panicked when she heard the shots and slammed on the brakes of the car, then ran into the theater for cover. Love was never implicated in the murder.

At first the police believed Buckley was murdered as a result of the successful recall of Mayor Bowles. Then word was passed along that Buckley was a racketeer in his own right. One rumor had it that Buckley was blackmailing gangsters by threatening exposure on the radio show if he wasn't paid to keep silent.

It was even said that Buckley offered to cease his attacks on the Bowles administration for a price. But the most prevalent theory was that he had double crossed the Eastside Mob. Buckley had been given $4000 to go to Ontario and arrange for a Canadian attorney to defend Eastside Mob leaders as a personal favor.

The mob leaders had been arrested on a concealed weapons charge and were facing serious prison time in Canada. The politically influential Buckley supposedly retained the attorney but Canadian exporters paid the lawyer to lose the case and Buckley was blamed.

Police believed that the same gangsters used the Bowles recall election as a smoke screen to take revenge on Buckley for the Canadian convictions.

Two suspects were arrested immediately. Jack Klein, a known Purple drug dealer, and another resident of the LaSalle Hotel named Angelo Livecchi. Klein was arrested because he was seated in the lobby when Buckley was shot to death, and had fled to his room. He was released when he said it happened so quickly that he "didn't see a thing."

Angelo Livecchi, however, was another story. He was an Eastside Mob gunman who shared a room at the LaSalle Hotel with Leonard "Black Leo" Cellura and Theodore Pizzino. He had been seen in the lobby of the LaSalle Hotel shortly before the first murders. Later he was found in bed, partially dressed, in his room at the hotel.

Collins and Cannon, victims of the first LaSalle murder, had tried to muscle in on Livecchi's roommate Theodore Pizzino and Leonard Cellura's club. Buckley had crossed Theodore Pizzino in the Canadian deal. It seemed that Livecchi had some extremely suspicious roommates.

Revelations about the once-revered Buckley piled up. A small-time bootlegger named Frank Chock signed an affidavit swearing that Buckley had set him up in the bootlegging business. Chock told Wayne County Prosecutor James Chenot that Buckley used his position in radio to muscle in on rackets.

He said the underworld regularly paid off Buckley to keep him from exposing their activities over his radio show. Chock later denied the story in an affidavit stating that he could not read English, and had put his signature on the first affidavit without knowing what he signed.

Wayne County Prosecutor James Chenot called for a twenty-three-man grand jury to investigate the Buckley murder and the rampant crime conditions in the city. This body quickly became popularly known as the "Buckley Grand Jury." They returned a blanket indictment charging among others Ted Pizzino and Angelo Livecchi.

The Buckley murder trial was scheduled to begin in 1931 with the most competent legal talent in the city representing the defendants. In the opening statement, prosecution claimed that the murder of Gerald Buckley was the result of his radio campaign against the Bowles administration and the underworld.

It was suggested that the defendants had financed Mayor Bowles's campaign. Prosecution also claimed the gangsters were protected by Bowles. The trial lasted six weeks in a standing room only courtroom.

When one witness' picture was taken by a courtroom photographer he refused to testify, telling the court that he feared for his life. His refusal to take the stand went a long way towards destroying the State's case as all other testimony was hearsay. After thirty-five hours, the jury acquitted all three defendants.

❖❖❖

The Purple Gang was also responding to the chaos and tension of intensified violence during the Great Depression. Earl Passman, identified by Detroit police as a bookkeeper for the Purple mob, was shot to death by another Purple gangster in an Owen Avenue apartment in a senseless shooting.

The apartment was being used as the headquarters for a whiskey delivery business. While several

Purples were in the kitchen taking telephone orders, Harry Altman, Harry Pont, and Passman sat in the living room drinking. Around 8:30 P.M., Altman got up to leave.

He noticed an open door and walked into the closet by mistake. Passman, a practical joker, seized the moment to play a prank on Altman. He jumped up and slammed the closet door shut, holding it tight. Pont ran up and helped Passman hold the door.

According to testimony by Pont, Altman yelled that if they didn't open the door he was going to shoot his way out. They thought Altman was joking. Suddenly a bullet splintered the closet door, striking Passman in the chest.

Not knowing what to do with the body, the men took it out to the alley behind the apartment building to make it look like Passman had been the victim of a drive-by shooting. At first, detectives thought that Passman was the victim of another underworld feud. Two days later, Harry Pont told detectives how Passman had really been killed.

In court Harry Pont refused to admit that he made a statement to police. The charges against Altman were dropped. Pont was held for contempt of court and given thirty days.

The gangsters were so tightly wound that they had simply become foolish. Purple gangsters were also encountering a new, serious problem. Witnesses were finally testifying against reputed Purple gangsters in open court.

It was the beginning of the end.

Chapter *9*

The Collingwood Manor Massacre

"These men checked their books with bullets and marked off their accounts with blood."

—Harry Toy,
Wayne County Prosecutor,
November 9, 1931

"I sat there in a daze while they killed those boys. It was awful. I lived a thousand lives. I walked out of there in a daze."

—Solly Levine,
November 11, 1931

The Collingwood Manor Massacre was the culmination of incidents that began in 1926, when three Chicago gunmen arrived in Detroit. Isadore Sutker, Joseph Lebovitz, and Herman Paul were minor thugs engaged in bootlegging and extortion during the mid-twenties, when Chicago mobs had begun to organize and the Capone organization vied for control of them.

109

At the time Sutker, Lebovitz, and Paul were racketeers engaged in bootlegging and small-scale extortion rackets. In 1925, the men had found their niche, shaking down Chicago speakeasy operators for protection money. Some speakeasy victims had gotten their beer from Capone suppliers and so were protected by the Capone syndicate.

When word reached Capone about them, Sutker, Lebovitz, and Paul were paid a visit. The gunmen were given a choice: they could leave Chicago voluntarily or be carried out in a box. Seeking greener—and safer—pastures, they left for Detroit.

There they became associated with members of the "Little Jewish Navy" faction of the Purple Gang, a group who operated out of a delicatessen and acquired their moniker from the member-owned speedboats used to run liquor from Canada. The operation was out of character for the Purple Gang. They usually preferred hijacking to high risk rum-running.

Sutker, Lebovitz, and Paul had met the Purple Gang through a peripheral Detroit underworld character named Solly Levine. Although Levine came from a well-to-do family, he had grown up with the original Purple gangsters and gone to grade school with the Bernstein brothers.

Levine worked legitimately at his father's business for a short time before succumbing to the lure of the underworld. He dabbled in all of the liquor related crimes, as a beer pusher, rumrunner, saloon owner, handbook operator and alcohol cutter. When Levine saw potential in the transplanted Chicago thugs, he introduced them to the Bernstein brothers.

The Purples allowed the three men to operate in a small area of the city in return for the customary kickbacks. But Sutker, Lebovitz, and Paul soon proved untrustworthy. They hijacked fellow Purple gangsters and preyed on other underworld operators, disregarding the territory of the other mobs.

They were so treacherous that no one dared to work with them, except Solly Levine who was tolerated because he bankrolled their underworld schemes. The trio became known as the Third Avenue Terrors. The three gunmen were attempting to establish themselves as an independent power in Purple Gang-controlled Detroit. By the late twenties, Lebovitz, Sutker, and Paul had signed their own death warrants by double dealing in the Detroit underworld.

When a Federal Prohibition agent was badly beaten by members of a downriver Italian mob and Feds cracked down on rum-running operations, it became necessary for the Italian mob to purchase alcohol from Detroit.

They approached the three Little Navy gangsters, assuming they were buying from the Purple-controlled alley brewing business, but Sutker, Lebovitz, and Paul purchased it from the Purples on credit and jacked up the price. They then began to muscle in on the Italian mob's customers.

By 1930 the three imported gunmen had begun shaking down Purple Gang-protected gambling and liquor rackets. Purple gangsters caught the trio's hired hands, who were taken for rides or forced to repay the money and leave town.

Still the Third Avenue Terrors refused to retreat. Sutker and Solly Levine opened a handbook operation as a front while Lebovitz and Paul operated a bootlegging business out of the back. Just before the Collingwood Massacre, the group had taken heavy losses in their handbook and were unable to pay off the winners.

To bail themselves out, they purchased $15,000 worth of alcohol from the Purples and several Italian mobs on credit. They planned to undercut local distributors and make up their losses by selling cut whiskey at an American Legion Convention in September of 1931.

Failure to pay off bets and undercutting the Purple Gang's liquor prices finally sealed their fate. The Purples decided it was time to do a little housecleaning. They had given Lebovitz, Sutker, and Paul their start and now had a responsibility to eliminate the problem. Ray Bernstein devised an elaborate scheme to set up the three men. The murders of Sutker, Lebovitz, and Paul had to be perfectly planned. They were seldom alone, always armed, and trusted nobody. Since they had tried to establish themselves as an independent power in the underworld, what they craved was recognition from the Purples that they had risen to the status of equals.

On August 18th, 1931, a man appeared at the manager's office of the Collingwood Manor Apartments on quiet, residential Collingwood Avenue. The stranger identified himself as James Regis and told the manager, Frank Holt, that he was interested in renting an apartment. He then returned two days later with $60— first month's rent—and was handed a set of keys to Apartment 211.

Bernstein decided to use Sol Levine as an unknowing accomplice to the plan. The arrangement appeared innocent enough. Ray Bernstein bumped into Levine in a deli. Bernstein told Levine that the Purples had decided to let him, Sutker, Lebovitz, and Paul be their agents in the liquor business.

They would handle wine, alcohol, and tickets (counterfeit liquor labels). The specifics would all be settled at a future meeting. Bernstein shook hands with Levine and told him that he would call in a couple of days to let him know where the meeting would be.

On September 16th, 1931, Ray Bernstein called the Selden Avenue handbook. He told Levine that a meeting had been arranged, and Levine was to bring his three partners to 1740 Collingwood Avenue.

All four men were unarmed when they entered the Collingwood apartments. As they walked into the lobby they were met by Ray Bernstein, who accompanied them to the apartment where they were greeted by Harry Fleisher, Harry Keywell, and Irving Milberg. The men shook hands and sat down.

The men engaged in lighthearted conversation. Sutker and Paul lit cigars. Suddenly, Ray Bernstein said, "Where's Scotty with the books?"

"Why don't you go down to the corner drugstore and call him," Fleisher suggested.

Bernstein's sedan was parked in the alley below. He started the car and raced the engine until it started backfiring. He then began blowing the horn.

Right on cue, Fleisher casually stood up, pulled a .38 caliber revolver from his coat and shot Lebovitz at point blank range. The bullet whizzed past Levine's nose, barely missing his head.

Milberg and Keywell jumped up and began shooting. Keywell emptied his revolver into Sutker, while Milberg shot Paul. Solly Levine froze in terror as the bullets flew by his head.

He watched helplessly as his three partners scrambled to their feet in a futile attempt to escape death. Paul and Lebovitz fell in a short hallway which led to a bedroom. Sutker, critically wounded, attempted to crawl under a bed.

In seconds, the gunfire ceased. Paul and Lebovitz lay face down in the growing pools of blood. Sutker lay on his side next to the bed. Fleisher wanted to kill Levine but Milberg and Keywell were against it. Ray Bernstein had given specific orders not to harm his friend.

All four men raced for the door, pausing to pitch their pistols into an open can of green paint. When they reached Bernstein in the waiting getaway car, Fleisher paused as if he had forgotten something. Suddenly, he ran back up the steps. Several more shots were fired.

When Fleisher got to the car the others looked at him in amazement. He told them that Lebovitz was still alive and he had to go back and finish him. The get-away car raced away.

After several blocks Ray Bernstein slammed on the brakes and Fleisher and Milberg jumped out. After several more blocks, Ray again stopped, and, turning to Levine, said "I'm your pal, Solly." He handed Levine several dollars for cab fare, "Go back to the book, Solly. We'll send a car for you later."

Levine stepped out, terrified and confused.

Meanwhile a tenant from the apartment below the scene of the massacre knocked on the super's door. She told him about the horrifying sounds and how a man had tore past her on the stairway. The super banged on the door of Apartment 211.

When there was no answer, he pushed the key into the lock and looked inside. As he stepped into the living room, he nearly tripped over the body of Joe Lebovitz. The floor of the apartment was covered in blood.

Horrified, Frank Holt, the building manager, slammed the apartment door and rushed to his apartment where he called the police. Within minutes, the detectives were on the scene of Detroit's worst gangland slayings since the Milaflores Apartment Massacre of '27.

"It sounded as if the ceiling were about to come down," one tenant told a detective. When she'd returned to her apartment, blood had begun to seep through the ceiling from the floor above.

When Levine got back to the handbook, he told several of his clients that Sutker, Lebovitz, and Paul had been kidnapped by unknown gunmen on their way to a meeting with Ray Bernstein.

He said he'd been told "We don't want you," and ordered to walk away and not look back. Once word of the Collingwood Massacre reached the Detroit police, the talkative Levine was arrested.

The Canfield detectives knew Levine to be a partner of the slain men and became a prime suspect in the murders. For awhile, Levine tenaciously stuck to his story: the three men had been kidnapped by unknown gangsters, and for some reason Solly was allowed to go free. Prosecutor Harry Toy suspected Levine as a fingerman.

The guns had been thrown into the paint cans by the killers to obliterate fingerprints. Their serial numbers were filed off, a common practice for murder weapons, but an acid etching test brought the serial numbers out. Ballistic tests proved that they were the same guns used to kill Sutker, Lebovitz, and Paul.

Tired and frightened, Solly confessed that he had been an eyewitness to the massacre. Levine then made a formal statement naming Harry Fleisher, Irving Milberg, and Harry Keywell as the shooters, and

Raymond Bernstein as the driver of the getaway car. Detectives were immediately dispatched with orders to bring the gunmen in dead or alive.

Later that day, Chief of Detectives, James McCarty, received an anonymous call. "Two of the men you want for the Collingwood murder are at 2649 Calvert. They will be out of town within the hour." Then the line went dead.

Heavily armed police rushed to 2649 Calvert and surrounded the house. It was owned by Charles Auerbach, a long-time underworld consultant and Purple Gang leader. Ray Bernstein and Harry Keywell were arrested in their pajamas.

Found in the house was $9025 in new fifty and hundred dollar bills, on Keywell's girlfriend; four .38 caliber revolvers; a .32 caliber automatic pistol; a 30-30 rifle and tear gas shells. Keywell and Bernstein were taken to police headquarters.

Irving Milberg was arrested the following night while preparing to leave town. He was taken to police headquarters with Fletcher and Axler and booked on the murder charge. Axler and Fletcher were held for investigation and released. Harry Fleisher was not found.

On September 21st, 1931, a warrant charging Ray Bernstein, Harry Keywell, Irving Milberg, and Harry Fleisher with the murder of Joseph Sutker was signed by Judge Edward Jeffries. On September 30th a frightened Sol Levine appeared for the pretrial examination. Levine named Raymond Bernstein, Harry Keywell, Irving Milberg, and Harry Fleisher as the Collingwood Massacre slayers.

During his hour of testimony, Levine looked solely at the prosecutor, avoiding the cold and deadly stares of the three defendants and the Purple gangsters in the spectators' gallery. The three defendants glared at Levine the whole time. Purple Gang defense lawyers failed to shake Levine's story.

Defense then made a motion for dismissal claiming that Levine's story could not be believed. The motion was bluntly denied by Judge Jeffries. He ordered the three men to be held without bond. On October 2nd, the three were arraigned before Judge Donald Van Zile.

The men stood mute on the charges of first degree murder, and a plea of not guilty was entered on their behalf. Extraordinary measures were taken to protect the State's star witness, Solly Levine. He was under a $500,000 bond at police headquarters, and guarded at all times by eight detectives.

Police searched everyone entering the courtroom. The city fire marshall limited the crowd of courtroom spectators to 500. The state planned to call a phenomenal fifty-two witnesses. It took four full days to pick the jury.

Over one hundred prospects were examined by attorneys. Judge Van Zile ordered the jury locked up after the selection process. The case would be tried by Wayne County Prosecutor Harry Toy and Assistant Prosecutor Miles Cullehan. Edward Kennedy Jr. and Rodney Baxter were to appear for the defense.

The day before the trial, the assistant prosecutor got a report that Purple Gang protected handbooks in the city were being squeezed for an extra two dollars a day to provide money for a defense fund. Detectives were ordered to bring in any bookmaker who would admit to being approached. None could be found.

On November 2, 1931, testimony in the Collingwood Massacre trial began. From the witness stand,

Solly Levine recited the events of his life, giving a brief biography and explaining how he had gotten involved with the underworld. He thought the meeting at the Collingwood Manor Apartments had been called to settle the alcohol debt between Ray Bernstein and his three partners, and claimed that he had no idea that he was taking the three men to their deaths.

Levine testified from 10:30 A.M. to 3:00 P.M., guarded by ten detectives. Four officers remained near Levine at all times while he was testifying. Levine believed that he would be killed right on the stand.

Even more was revealed the second day of the trial. Harry McDonald, the caretaker across the alley from the Collingwood Manor Apartments, testified for the State. He had been standing in his kitchen when his attention was attracted to Bernstein's car. He related how the motor racing and the horn blowing were followed by a volley of shots.

He also saw the four men run out of the building. When asked by the prosecution if he could identify the driver, McDonald walked over to Ray Bernstein and put his hand on Bernstein's shoulder. McDonald even placed the time of the incident.

The defense continued to concentrate on what they called Sol Levine's lack of credibility. The jury was taken to the scene of the slayings. The defendants, handcuffed to each other, stood by and watched while police armed with Thompson submachine guns guarded the alley.

At Apartment 211 the positions in which the bodies were found and bullet fragments from the shootings were presented as evidence. The jurors were taken to and from the apartment in a heavily guarded city bus followed by a patrol wagon carrying the defendants. Five carloads of detectives brought up the rear.

Witness after witness took the stand, claiming sightings of the getaway car, although at least one perjured earlier testimony. Before giving the case to the jury, the State made an effort to prove that Ray Bernstein was the man who had posed as James Regis when he rented Apartment 211 the previous August.

The whole case was circumstantial, dependent upon whether Levine's testimony was believable. The only argument the defense had was that Levine himself was actually involved in the murder plot.

A verdict in the Collingwood Manor Massacre case was returned in one hour and thirty-seven minutes. All three defendants were found guilty of first degree murder. Pandemonium erupted in the courtroom, while relatives and friends of the defendants became hysterical.

Chief of Detectives James E. McCarty later commented to the press, "This conviction is the greatest accomplishment . . . in years. Not only does it break the back of the Purple Gang but it serves notice on other mobs that murder doesn't go anymore in Detroit."

The three convicted Purples were sentenced to life in Marquette Prison without parole. This was the first time that Bernstein or Keywell had ever faced a jury on a murder charge.

The Collingwood Manor Massacre turned Detroit around. There was a major law enforcement crackdown in its aftermath. As a result, gangsters turned into entrepreneurs.

"One-Armed" Mike Gelfand developed a novel idea. In August of 1931, Gelfand's sister Lillian had been given eighty acres of land in Michigan. Here, Gelfand planned to build a remote haven to be used by Detroit gangsters on the lam. Gelfand's sister sold him the property for one dollar.

He and his wife moved to the area and had plans drawn up for a restaurant and dancing pavilion to cater to local residents while providing a safe house for gangster fugitives. It would become known as the Famous Graceland Ballroom.

During its heyday in the mid-thirties, the resort boasted a runway for small aircraft, tourist cabins, and three tunnels, used by fugitives to escape into the nearby woods. The place was visited by many notorious Purple gangsters, as well as underworld characters from all over the Midwest.

The same week that the Collingwood Massacre shocked the citizens of Detroit, the State's new Public Enemy Law became effective. The main thrust of the law was to attack underworld mobs like the Purple Gang by making it a crime to be associated with any organization which engaged in an illegal occupation or business. Officially known as the Disorderly Persons Act, State legislators were hopeful that the new law would drive hoodlums out of Michigan.

For political corruption, it imposed fines and jail sentences on bondsmen and criminal attorneys who loitered around police stations, court buildings, hospitals, etc., soliciting criminals. For the actual gangsters, all the State required was proof of an individual's reputation. Any person convicted would be guilty of a misdemeanor and fined $100 or 90 days in jail, a second conviction could bring a $100 fine and six months in jail, and a third conviction could mean a fine and two years in prison.

The first local characters to be tried under the law were Purples picked up in a dragnet following the Collingwood Massacre. Charles "The Professor" Auerbach, in whose home Keywell and Bernstein were arrested, was held as a public enemy along with Abe Axler and Eddie Fletcher. In the warrants Axler and Fletcher were charged with "having joined with other gangsters and confederated into an illegal group commonly known by the name Purple Gang, conducting illegal business. . . ."

Auerbach was charged with "having in his possession unregistered guns and tear gas bombs for the purpose of unlawfully distributing them." The three men were arraigned and pleaded not guilty, requesting a jury trial. They were released on bonds of $500 each.

Abe Axler's trial opened on October 5, 1931—the first ever under the Public Enemy Law—with a three hour argument between defense attorney Edward Kennedy Jr., and County Prosecutor George S. Fitzgerald. Kennedy argued that any actions of Axler before the law became effective were out of bounds.

The State attempted to prove the gangster's reputation with police testimony, his criminal record and press notices. The second day was spent arguing the constitutionality of the new law. Twice Kennedy made a motion for a mistrial.

After deliberating for three hours and thirty-seven minutes, the jury brought in a "not guilty" verdict. Undeterred by the results of the Axler trial, Fitzgerald declared that he would prosecute Fletcher, Auerbach, and other Purple gangsters held on similar charges.

Cases against Eddie Fletcher, Harry Millman, and Morris Raider were later dismissed because the State had had no criminal charges against these men since September 18, 1931, and they could not be tried for crimes committed before the Act took effect. But it was already too late for the original Purple gang, they were suffering the final blows.

In late 1931 the so-called Junior Purple Gang was to make its debut in the Detroit underworld. This was a group several years younger than the Purple Gang. But only one, a flashy, clever wise guy named Myron "Mikey" Selik, would approach the notoriety of some of the original Purple gangsters.

On October 8, 1931, Selik, Irving Feldman, Sollie Isaacs, and Robert Goldstein held up a handbook located in the basement of a restaurant. The four casually walked into the building and went to the basement as if to place a bet. About thirty men were present when Selik, Isaacs, and Goldstein produced revolvers and ordered the occupants to line up facing the wall.

Goldstein searched the victims while the others kept them covered. The bandits collected the grand total of $225 worth of loot including some jewelry and several pistols. One man who had escaped the robbery in the confusion ran down Monroe Street yelling "stick up!"

His plea for help attracted the attention of a nearby patrolman who accompanied the man back to the restaurant. The chef showed the police officer the stairway to the basement handbook. When the patrolman arrived on the scene, he found the robbery in progress. The officer ordered the bandits to drop their guns, which the inexperienced outlaws quickly did. Upon arresting the men, pistols were found in all of their pockets.

Selik alone had three guns in his overcoat and pants. He was sentenced to six to twelve years in the Michigan State Reformatory and would spend most of the next 30 years in and out of State prisons.

Unlike the first wave of Purples, Selik was born into an affluent home. His father owned a successful machine shop which prospered during World War I. His parents split in the early twenties, the result of his father's infidelity and gambling.

Selik spent most of his time on the street, left school in the tenth grade, and drifted from one job to another. He began gambling and hanging around poolrooms frequented by Purple members. Selik admired the now aging gangsters and began to emulate them in dress and behavior.

He later told a prison social worker that "only suckers work." But the beginning of a younger Purple Gang was the era of decline for the real thing. They saw the end of their reign with the murder of Milford Jones.

For nearly fifteen years Milford Jones terrorized the midwestern underworld. As a youngster Jones had been a gunman for the ruthless Egan's Rats Mob. In later years he gained notoriety as a freelance killer, bank robber, and kidnapper; one who'd participated in a number of kidnapping plots with Purple gangsters.

He based his reputation as a professional killer on the fact that he'd run many Sicilian and Italian mobsters out of St. Louis, or killed those who refused to leave. By 1930 many former St. Louis gangsters were living in Detroit, and they feared and hated Jones.

At 4 A.M. on June 15th, 1932, Jones stepped up to the bar of the glamourous Stork Club. Four well dressed men stood quietly at the other end. Jones greeted the men and turned to order a drink. In the mirror, Jones watched helplessly as the men pulled pistols.

Realizing that he was about to be "hit," Jones jerked his jacket up over his head and made a plea for mercy, barely audible above the roar of pistols. Jones collapsed in a heap at the bar, his legs tangled in its rail.

The police were not notified for more than three

hours. Gunfire had caused the patrons and the band to panic. Unfinished meals were on the tables and instruments thrown to the floor as the crowd dashed for the door.

The only person in the place when police arrived was the owner, Jack Green. He'd placed the call to police headquarters by telling them he had a dead man in his club.

At the time of his death, Milford Jones was operating a cabaret in St. Louis. He was reported to have been supplying his club through his long time connections with the Purple Gang. The rumor was that Jones was in Detroit on a contract with Irish gangsters to drive Thomas "Yonny" Licavoli out of Ohio for strong-arming competing mobsters out of bootlegging and other lucrative rackets.

Jones had a fearsome reputation. It was even reported that he had called Licavoli when he arrived in Detroit and said, "Get your mob out of Toledo or I'll come down there and get you out."

In Jones, the Purple Gang had had an important underworld ally. The loss of any freelance strong arm man weakened the foundation of the skeleton crew that made up the actual Purple Gang. Without outside muscle, they were vulnerable to those who wanted to topple the former underworld power.

At 6:15 that same morning a sixteen-year-old boy found a .38 caliber Smith and Wesson revolver. Six empty shells were in the chambers. He was afraid to turn the weapon over to police after news of the murder was out. After communicating with a friend who knew detectives on the Special Investigations Squad, the weapon was turned over to police. Ballistics tests indicated that the gun was one of the weapons used to kill Jones. Both Jack Green and Peter Gorenfield, principal owners of the Stork Club, denied admitting Jones or any of the four murder suspects to the club. Admittance to the cabaret was by card only.

Supposedly, by this system anyone who entered was either vouched for by friends or known by the proprietors or employees. Green and Gorenfield were held for questioning as police witnesses. Several other Stork Club employees and known patrons were also picked up and questioned by police. Witnesses positively identified two of the gunmen from mug shot photographs at police headquarters. The two suspects turned out to be local gangsters and members of the Eastside Mob. They were named as Pete Licavoli and Joe Massei. Detroit police were also searching for Joe "Scarface" Bommarito and Pete Corrado, both known gunmen who they believed had accompanied Licavoli and Massei to the Stork Club the night Jones was murdered.

The cases against Pete Licavoli and Joe Massei for the Jones' slaying were eventually dropped. Massei was finally arrested in Detroit on the original murder charge on February 2, 1933. Pete Licavoli was arrested on May 2, 1933. The charges were dismissed after Peter Gorenfield jumped a $5000 bond as a police witness and disappeared. Jack Green, also held as a witness, was released because of the Court's inability to locate Gorenfield.

In the meantime, the Purples' leaders were all in jail. The Collingwood massacre trial defense team had been working on a legal strategy to free Ray Bernstein, Irving Milberg, and Harry Keywell. Immediately after the convictions of these three in the Collingwood Manor Massacre case, the Purples' chief lawyer, Edward Kennedy Jr., filed an appeal with the Michigan Supreme Court.

The original appeal was still pending in March of 1932 when defense attorney Henry Meyers filed a motion for a new trial.

The defense team had been told that if new evidence surfaced they should proceed with such a motion. It was the beginning of a long legal battle to free the three men. Meyers was one of a team of attorneys retained by the families of the convicted trio. The new defense motion was based on information presented in an affidavit purportedly made by Solly Levine.

Levine had been the prosecution's star witness in the original murder trial and the only eyewitness to the murders. He had gone into hiding immediately after the Collingwood Massacre trial ended. Levine now claimed that Bernstein, Milberg, Keywell, and Fleisher were not the killers. According to him, he had been forced to testify by the police and the County Prosecutor's Office.

Wayne County Prosecutor Harry Toy filed ten reasons why Meyers's new motion should be quashed by the court. Toy's main argument was that Judge Donald Van Zile no longer had the jurisdiction to grant the men a new trial. The statutory period during which such an appeal could be made had expired on December 10th, 1931.

Original jurisdiction in the case had passed to the Michigan Supreme Court, where the motion filed in January of 1932 was still pending. Judge Van Zile had presided over the original murder trial and sentenced the three gangsters in the case. The affidavit from Levine had been received the previous week. In it Levine swore that he did not know who the actual killers were but that he could identify them if he ever saw them again.

Levine also promised to repudiate his original trial testimony. In the affidavit Levine said that Detroit police had tortured him to obtain a confession.

At first, according to Levine, detectives had tried to force him to name Abe Axler, Joe "Honey" Miller, and Isadore Bernstein as the killers. After grilling Levine for many hours without food or sleep, the police named Ray Bernstein, Harry Keywell, Irv Milberg, and Harry Fleisher as the prime suspects in the massacre. When Levine objected, he was told that if he did not name the four he would be charged with the slayings and go to prison for life.

Levine wrote in a letter that after the trial Detectives Earl Switzer and Harold Branton took him to Alabama. Levine was then put on a France-bound ship under the name of Fred Schultz. When he arrived in the country he was refused admission and returned to the United States. On February 3rd, 1932, his ship landed in Norfolk, Virginia, where he was met by his mother, sister, and detectives Switzer and Branton. At this time Levine stated that he told the two police officers that he was going back to Detroit to "tell the truth." Levine was then forced to accompany the two police officers to Washington, where a passport was obtained for him in his own name.

Levine claimed the police wanted him to go back to Europe but he refused. He then added that they started out for Oklahoma City. While passing through some swampland, the two detectives stopped the car and threatened Levine that they would kill him and throw his body in the swamp if he did not give them a statement when they reached Oklahoma City. They arrived in Oklahoma City on February 13th, 1932. Under threat, he signed statements, presented to him by the two detectives, which said that Bernstein, Milberg, Keywell, and Fleisher were the shooters in the Collingwood Massacre.

The new affidavit in the possession of defense attorney Meyers was sworn to be true and in Levine's words, "made freely and voluntarily to clear my conscience because I realized a great injustice had been inflicted on the three men." Shortly after Levine's statement was filed, another affidavit was filed by his sister. In this affidavit she swore that on September 18th, 1931, two days after Levine was arrested as a police witness, she saw her brother in the office of Judge John A. Boyne. At this time Levine opened his shirt and she saw that his upper body was black and blue with bruises from his police interrogation. Four hours later Mrs. Edelson saw her brother again. His ears red and inflamed, he told her that police had held a lit cigar behind them.

On March 18th the motion for a new trial was denied by Judge Donald Van Zile on the grounds that he had lost jurisdiction in the case. In October the Michigan Supreme Court finally ruled on the appeal and upheld the convictions of Bernstein, Keywell, and Milberg.

At 10:15 A.M. on June 9th, 1932, Harry Fleisher, the subject of a nationwide manhunt for the previous nine months, strolled casually into the office of Wayne County Prosecutor Harry Toy and surrendered on the Collingwood Massacre murder warrant, accompanied by his attorneys, Edward Kennedy Jr. and William Friedman. Both Kennedy and Friedman had participated in the defense of the three Purple gangsters convicted in the Collingwood Massacre trial. Toy was shocked when he saw Fleisher step from the elevator on the fifth floor of police headquarters, dressed in a new blue suit and grinning from ear to ear.

Kennedy presented a written statement to the dumb-founded prosecutor that Fleisher had turned himself in to help free Bernstein, Keywell, and Milberg. For the previous nine months while Fleisher had been on the lam, he had been named as a suspect in almost every crime of importance, including the kidnapping of the Lindbergh baby.

The suspicions were not unfounded. Fleisher had a record as a kidnapper not only in Detroit but in other cities. In February of 1930 Fleisher and another gangster named Sam "Lefty" Handel were picked up in New York for the kidnapping of a wealthy Connecticut Realtor named Max Price. A $30,000 ransom had been demanded and Price ordered killed when the money was not forthcoming. After being held prisoner for nine days, Price was released unharmed. Max Price and a friend later identified Fleisher and Handel as two of the four men who abducted him from his New Haven home in January of 1930. A neighbor of Price identified Fleisher as the man who physically over-powered Price and threw him in the car. Both Fleisher and Handel were arrested and later released when witnesses refused to testify.

Harry Fleisher had been on the run since June 1st, 1931, three months before the Collingwood Massacre. At that time he had been indicted for conspiracy to violate the Federal Prohibition Law. The indictment grew out of a Federal raid on the Leonard Warehouse in Detroit. Federal agents had found a huge distilling plant set up and operated by a number of Purple gangsters. The investigation had begun with a fire.

On January 3rd, 1931, the building mysteriously burst into flames. Firemen responding to the blaze discovered the huge brewing plant. Prohibition agents working on the case later disclosed that the equipment in the plant was valued at more than $150,000. This equipment was later sold off at a police auction. Harry Fleisher, Henry Shorr, Jack Grendal, Harry Harris, Louis Gellerman, and John Silvers were named in the Federal indictment.

The addresses of the men were given as the Oakland Sugar House. Shorr had purchased the brewery equipment in New York and had it shipped to the Eastside Waste Paper Company, reported to be owned by Harry Fleisher.

Following Fleisher's arrest for the Collingwood Massacre, he was interrogated at police headquarters by three F.B.I. agents. They wanted to question him to see if he had any information about the Lindbergh kidnapping. According to a letter to the Director from the Special Agent in Charge of the Detroit office, the Feds believed that Fleisher had been reached by his attorney prior to his surrender. The agent in charge, Larsen, had been one of the Feds who interrogated Fleisher. Larsen claimed that during the questioning Fleisher did not become "hard boiled" but carefully avoided answering specific questions put to him.

When asked about the actions of the Purple Gang, Fleisher denied knowing any of them intimately. "A lot of fellows claim to know me, but I don't know them," explained Fleisher. Officials involved in the Collingwood Manor Massacre investigations believed that Purple Gang lawyers had Fleisher surrender when they felt that the State lacked witnesses to convict him.

When questioned about the Price kidnapping in 1930, Fleisher claimed he knew nothing about it. He had been visiting New York for a few days when he was picked up by police. Fleisher was also questioned by Detective Frank Carr of the Newark Police and Louis Bornman of the New Jersey State Police about the Lindbergh kidnapping.

Throughout the interrogation Fleisher remained cordial but responded to most questions with a smile and a shrug. Fleisher's attorneys claimed that his surrender would prove the innocence of the three convicted Purple gangsters in the Collingwood Massacre case. Fleisher had an alibi; he was locked up in the Reading, Pennsylvania jail the day of the murders. Fleisher had been named by Levine as one of the gunmen. If he was not there, surely this would cast a long shadow of doubt on the guilt of the three convicted killers. After what was essentially a useless grilling, Fleisher was locked up at police headquarters.

On June 21st, 1932, an indictment charging Fleisher with the Collingwood Manor Massacre was handed down by a Wayne County Grand Jury. Fleisher was held without bond in the Wayne County Jail pending jury action. Before Fleisher's examination on the charge there was some confusion as to why Prosecutor Toy wanted to transfer the case from Recorders Court to Wayne County Circuit Court. Toy claimed it was because of the pending Grand Jury indictment but Judge Jeffries insisted that the case be based on the original warrant and tried in Recorders Court.

On June 25th, 1932, a motion was made to allow a transcript of Levine's testimony from the Collingwood Massacre trial to be used if Solly Levine could not be found. When Toy asked for an adjournment of the hearing to search for Levine, defense attorneys presented a motion for dismissal of the case. This motion was denied.

Fleisher was arraigned on June 27th, 1932, and pleaded not guilty to the specific charge of murdering Isadore Sutker. Edward Kennedy Jr. later asked the court if Harry Fleisher's plea of not guilty could be changed to a plea of not guilty by standing mute. This motion was allowed. Several more examination dates and adjournments transpired. Finally, on July 25, 1932, Prosecutor Harry Toy admitted to Judge Thomas Cotter that Solly Levine could not be found. Toy was about to make a motion for dismissal of the case based on lack of evidence when the Judge suggested that Levine's testimony in the original trial be used against Fleisher.

After Fleisher was arraigned on the original murder warrant, he was indicted by the grand jury for the same crime. This only magnified the procedural confusion already surrounding the case. The legal question posed by Judge Cotter was whether testimony used to convict three of the defendants in the original trial could be used against another defendant, specifically if that defendant, Harry Fleisher, was not present at the original trial to refute the testimony. On July 25th, 1932, the Fleisher case examination was again postponed because Solly Levine could not be found. Cotter threatened defense attorneys, telling them that they were guilty of tampering with justice if they were concealing Levine's whereabouts. Cotter argued that Levine's presence was not really necessary to proceed because Fleisher was in hiding at the time of the Collingwood Manor Massacre trial. The judge noted that because Fleisher failed to appear in court to refute Levine's testimony, he saw no reason why the original court record could not be used against Fleisher at his trial.

The chances of officials finding Solly Levine were remote. It had even been rumored that a relative of one of the convicted Purple gangsters had traveled to Oklahoma City to see Levine in regard to the affidavit which recanted his original testimony. When Levine found this out he quit his job and left the city. Fleisher's legal counsel continued to deny that they had any knowledge regarding his whereabouts.

On August 1st, 1932, Fleisher's trial was again adjourned as the result of a request by Toy, who was still unable to locate Levine. Toy explained to Van Zile that he wanted to exhaust every angle to find the missing witness. This adjournment was vehemently protested by Edward Kennedy Jr., who denounced the courtroom tactics as a ruse to prevent Fleisher from his constitutional right to a speedy and immediate trial. Kennedy correctly argued that it had been Toy himself who was responsible for Levine being in hiding and out of the jurisdiction of the court. Kennedy's objection was overruled.

Toy finally established that the court could not use the testimony of the original murder trial against Fleisher. The only way that this procedure was legal was if the court could prove Fleisher was directly preventing Solly Levine from returning to testify. The defense continued to argue that Fleisher had spent September 16th, 1931 in a Reading, Pennsylvania jail cell.

The murder trial of Harry Fleisher opened before Judge Henry S. Sweeny in Detroit Recorders Court on September 7th, 1932. At the start of the trial Toy made a motion for dismissal of the case against Fleisher based on a legal motion of nolle prosequi (dismissal of the case without prejudice). Toy charged in his state-

ment that organized gangdom had effectively prevented
Sol Levine from testifying against Fleisher. Edward
Kennedy Jr. opposed the nolle prosequi motion stating that Fleisher should have the right of a speedy trial.
The case was sent to Judge Edward Jefferies, the pre-
siding Chief Judge. Jeffries then dismissed the case
on the nolle prosequi motion. Fleisher was immediately turned over to the U.S. Marshal's office on the
Leonard Warehouse indictment.

In his motion to dismiss Prosecutor Toy argued that
stenographers' notes on Solly Levine's testimony used
in the original trial to convict Keywell, Bernstein, and
Milberg could not be used against Harry Fleisher. Under
Michigan law Fleisher would have had to be present
for Levine's original testimony. The defendant was enti-
tled to the right of confronting and cross examining
the witness, as required by the Michigan Constitution
as well as the Constitution of the United States in all
criminal cases.

Toy emphasized that Fleisher had surrendered to
authorities only after Sol Levine could not be located.
Toy noted that police officials believed Levine's absence
was caused by gang associates of Harry Fleisher. The
prosecutor believed that if the State went to trial it
could not win the case against Fleisher. If other evidence was discovered at a later date or if Levine
appeared, Fleisher would never again be able to be
tried for the murders, as he would then be placed in
double jeopardy. The only thing left to do in Toy's
opinion was to dismiss the indictment without prejudice, essentially leaving the case open. If evidence
could be found at a later date, Fleisher could still be
charged on the original murder warrant.

In October of 1932, the Michigan Supreme Court

upheld the murder convictions of Bernstein, Keywell, and Milberg. In the official statement handed down by the court, Purple attorney Edward Kennedy Jr. was authorized to ask Judge Donald Van Zile to reopen the case if new evidence was uncovered.

In April of 1933, Kennedy submitted a request to Judge Van Zile to allow New York attorney Fred D. Kaplan to be admitted to practice law in Detroit. This was in preparation for filing a second motion for a new trial in the Collingwood case. Kaplan would appear in court as a new part of the Purple defense team if for some reason Kennedy could not. He was admitted by Judge Van Zile.

Kaplan was a former law partner of New York criminal attorney Isiah Leebove. Leebove had caused a sensation of his own in Michigan when he sought a private meeting with Bernstein, Milberg, and Keywell in Marquette Prison. Having recently been named a special advisor to Governor William Comstock. It was widely believed that he was going to use his political influence with the governor to get a new trial for the convicted Purple gangsters.

Leebove had already gained notoriety in New York by successfully defending a number of major New York mobsters, including Arnold Rothstein, "Legs" Diamond, and "Dapper" Don Collins. He was a principal contributor to the Comstock gubernatorial campaign. After the election Leebove was appointed by the governor to make a study of the Michigan prison system and recommend cost cutting changes. His former law partner, Fred Kaplan, was retained by Joe Bernstein.

The second motion for a new trial in the massacre case was filed on Monday, July 16, 1933, by Edward

Kennedy Jr. The motion was based on thirty affidavits, three of which were from the prisoners themselves and another from a former Reading, Pennsylvania police officer.

The affidavits were comprised of 156 pages of supposedly new alibi evidence. Essentially, the new information claimed that Harry Keywell and Ray Bernstein were placing telephone bets with bookmakers around the country on the afternoon of September 16th, 1931, when the massacre took place. These bets were made from the home of Bernstein's sister, Mrs. Jean Winston. Irving Milberg stated that he was in bed most of the day, and Harry Fleisher spent that day and night in a Reading, Pennsylvania jail cell. The nature of the alibis presented in the motion for a new trial demonstrated the tremendous influence that the Purple Gang wielded at the time. This influence was not only local but included important contacts in the national underworld.

In a statement to the court, Abe Bernstein claimed that he had obtained long distance telephone records from a former superintendent of the Michigan Bell Telephone Company named Lou Bert, supposedly Bernstein's personal friend. These phone slips showed that long distance phone calls had been placed from the Bernsteins' sister's home on the afternoon of September 16, 1931, to Cincinnati, Chicago, and New York.

They had been made between the hours of 2:00 P.M. and 4:00 P.M. (the massacre occurred between 3:25 and 3:30 P.M. on the 16th). Bernstein explained that the phone slips, documenting a $1200 horse bet, had not been mentioned in the original Massacre trial because he had misplaced them. They were not found, according to Bernstein, until April of 1932.

The phone company superintendent died shortly before the Collingwood trial began. Abe Bernstein now claimed that if this had not happened he would have been able to produce the telephone records sooner. Additional affidavits were presented to substantiate Abe Bernstein's statement. These statements were signed by out-of-town bookies. The bookmakers stated that they had accepted bets from Ray Bernstein and Harry Keywell on the date and times mentioned in Abe Bernstein's information. Milberg and his wife Bertha swore in their affidavit that they had been up all night playing cards until 7:30 on the morning of September 16, 1931. They then went to bed and did not get up until 3:30 that afternoon. Harry Fleisher was reported to have spent the night in a Reading, Pennsylvania jail under the name of Harry Fishman.

A signature on the Reading jail arrest ticket for September 16, 1931, perfectly matched Fleisher's handwriting sample. Kennedy was asked by the court why the phone call evidence offered by Abe Bernstein was not presented as information in the original Massacre trial. Kennedy claimed that because Bert had died the day before testimony was to be taken, duplicate phone call receipts could not be produced. Kennedy told the court that he thought if Abe Bernstein had testified that he had lost the original receipts in his possession, it would have looked ridiculous to a jury. Therefore, he chose not to use the alibi evidence. Kennedy was then asked by the court why he did not include the evidence of the telephone calls when he filed the first motion for a new trial. Abe Bernstein had supposedly found the misplaced slips again that April. Kennedy had no answer to this question.

On August 8th, 1933, Harry Fleisher was introduced as the first alibi witness. Defense attorney Kaplan told the court that by establishing Fleisher's innocence in the Collingwood affair he hoped to introduce new evidence in favor of the three convicted Purples and their legal struggle for a new trial. Kaplan further argued that the original evidence used to arrest Bernstein, Milberg, and Keywell was insufficient as no one had identified the three Purples, not even Solly Levine. According to Kaplan, Levine had been subjected to torture at the hands of the police and did not recall himself whether he had identified any of the defendants during the initial questioning.

Kaplan pointed out that even as late as September 18th, 1931, Toy had spoken of five men leaving the murder scene and was not sure if Solly Levine was one of them. Kaplan also presented an affidavit in which Levine denied all previous statements and again claimed that he was forced by the police to name the four Purples in the murders. This affidavit was supposedly substantiated by a police prisoner in the cell next to Levine's during the interrogations. This man claimed that Levine had been beaten and brutalized by police. He further stated that Levine told him police tried to force him to implicate more Purple gangsters in the Collingwood murders, including Abe Axler and Joe "Honey" Miller.

That same day the prosecutor began blowing holes in the defense alibi affidavits. The lost telephone receipts that had been provided by Abe Bernstein were discredited by a Bell Telephone Supervisor named Joseph Brett and by Superintendent Burt's former secretary. Both Bell employees stated that they had never met Abe Bernstein before and had never seen the phone slips presented by the defense. They also destroyed the defense team's argument that the lost telephone slips could not be duplicated. Both testified that all telephone record slips were held by the company for six months and then destroyed. Bernstein could have obtained copies of the slips on request at any time during the six month period, without having to secret them out of telephone company files. Toy argued that if Bernstein had really lost the slips as he claimed, the defense could have easily gotten duplicates.

Toy also destroyed the Milbergs' alibi. In an affidavit given shortly after the massacre, the Milbergs' maid claimed Irving Milberg left home shortly after noon on September 16, 1931, and did not return until 6:00 P.M. She also added that when Milberg returned home he was too nervous to eat dinner. Mrs. Milberg found out that the maid made a statement to Detroit police and promptly fired her. She claimed that several days later she was approached by Mrs. Milberg and a man she did not know, and offered $130 plus back pay if she would stay away from the trial and not testify. The maid agreed not to testify for fear that she or her child would be harmed.

Affidavits from two former Reading, Pennsylvania police officers presented by the defense were also successfully refuted by Toy. The first affidavit presented by the prosecutor was from J. Stanley Giles, the Reading Police Commissioner. In the affidavit Giles explained that all records of arrests were first entered on a yellow sheet in long hand then typed onto a pink sheet when placed in the official records. The name Fishman (Fleisher's alias when he was arrested) did not appear on any yellow sheet for the week in question. The name, however, had been found on a pink sheet dated September 18th, 1931, that had obviously been tampered with. Another affidavit was presented by Toy from a Sergeant Jacob Rapp of the Reading police. Rapp claimed that there was no arrest record of any man named Fishman in the docket during the time in question. A police clerk named Deem swore in another affidavit that he had searched the records from September 9th, 1931 to December 31st, 1931. He found no record of the arrest of a man named Fleisher or Fishman. Deem claimed that he personally typed all of the pink sheets. The one that was presented by Purple Gang defense attorneys was not typed by him and was in fact typed on a different typewriter than the machines normally used by the department. Deem said that in his opinion the original sheet had been removed from the book and replaced by another sheet bearing Fleisher's signature using the alias "Fishman."

The most incriminating affidavit refuting Fleisher's alibi came from Samuel Kirchoff. Kirchoff was a guard at the Reading jail. He worked the midnight shift from midnight to 8:00 A.M. and had never seen Harry Fleisher in his jail. He would have remembered him if he had. He also had no recollection of a man named Fishman arrested on the date mentioned by the defense. Kirchoff did acknowledge, however, that on October 23th, 1931, the acting captain of detectives came to him and told him that there had been a mistake in the records. He then ordered Kirchoff to make out two arrest record tickets for two persons he claimed were arrested a month or so before and to date them September 16th, 1931. Acting captain Dentith then took the tickets with the signatures of the prisoners left blank. Kirchoff asserted that this incident was the only time in his eighteen years as a jail guard that he was ever asked to make out an arrest ticket after the day of the actual arrest.

Both Charles Dentith, the former Reading detective lieutenant, and Fred Marks, head of the Berks County Pennsylvania detective force, were brought to Detroit by the defense team and introduced as witnesses to refute the charge that Fleisher's alibi evidence was manufactured. Marks was to testify that he had been called to the jail to look at a prisoner named Harry Fishman, who in reality was Harry Fleisher. Neither was allowed to testify.

Detective John R. Machlik of the Detroit police presented an affidavit that he had talked with Detective Marks a year before in Reading. At that time Marks told him that he had met Abe and Ray Bernstein in a New York hotel and that he was acquainted with a Reading man named Max Hassel. Hassel at that time was a powerful bootlegger in Pennsylvania and New Jersey. He also owned a hotel in Reading.

It was on the street corner in front of this hotel that Harry Fleisher was supposedly arrested on September 16, 1931. Since that time both Dentith and Marks had been discharged from the police force. Dentith acted as a personal bodyguard for Max Hassel, a New York Syndicate member, up until his murder. Hassel was connected with mobster "Waxey" Gordon and Alex Greenberg, who controlled over twenty of the New York underworld's major breweries.

On April 12, 1933, Greenberg and Hassel were murdered in their beds at the Cartaret Hotel in Elizabeth, New Jersey. Gordon miraculously escaped. Police believed that the two men were possibly set up by Gordon himself. Detective Marks coincidentally had two brothers in Detroit who ran handbooks, which at that time were under the protection and control of the Purple Gang.

The final affidavit refuting Harry Fleisher's alibi was from Patrolman Albert Bice of the Bethune Avenue Station. Bice claimed that he had seen and spoken to Harry Fleisher on the morning of September 17th, 1931. This was the day after the massacre. He saw Fleisher at the corner of Clairmount and Woodward Avenue. According to Bice, when he spoke to Fleisher he responded with a wave of his hand. The next day when a teletype came into the station naming Fleisher as a suspect in the massacre, Bice mentioned to his superior that he had seen Fleisher the previous day. He was reprimanded because he had failed to arrest Fleisher on the outstanding Federal warrant charging him with Prohibition violation in the Leonard Warehouse case.

Bice admitted that he had known Harry Fleisher for years. His testimony was in direct contradiction to Fleisher's statement claiming that he had been released from the Reading jail at 7:30 A.M. on September 17th, 1931. The patrolman claimed that he had seen and spoken to Fleisher at 10:30 that same morning.

On October 6th, 1933, Judge Van Zile denied the Purples' defense attorneys' request for a new trial. Van Zile ruled out the alibi affidavits as "surely not newly discovered evidence," adding that "they did not impress the court as the truth." The judge also stated that Levine's story was unbelievable.

It is interesting to note how the Purples were able to pull strings with the Eastern mob through Max Hassel. Through gang connections a corrupt high ranking Reading police official was able to insert alibi evidence into the official records of the Reading Police Department placing Fleisher in jail the day of the massacre.

Abe Bernstein through his contacts was also able

to get bookmakers in New York, Cincinnati, and Chicago to give sworn affidavits that they had been on the phone with Ray Bernstein and Keywell taking bets at the time that the massacre was taking place. The Purple Gang defense team was even able to get an affidavit from a Detroit bookmaker named Jacob Silverman. Silverman claimed that he had set up Sutker, Lebowitz, and Paul (the massacre victims) in a Selden Avenue handbook business. Silverman said that Sutker owed him money and claimed that Sutker told him on the day of the massacre that he and his partners had a Sept 16th meeting with some Italian bookmakers from Toledo.

By 1933, long prison sentences and inter-gang sniping continued to destroy the gang. In November of 1933, two Purple Gang lieutenants, Abe Axler and Eddie Fletcher, were mysteriously shot to death, their bodies left on a lonely Oakland County road. The murder of such powerful Purples had previously been unimaginable.

Chapter *10*

The Self-Destruction

"The deliberate 'execution' of two notorious gangsters serves to remind us of the fact that a criminal career runs always to the same finish. Yet it runs for too long with society helpless to put a stop to it."

—*Detroit Times* Editorial,
November 28, 1933

"I'm through with the racket for keeps."

—Abe Axler, Purple gangster,
November 1933

Early one morning in November 1933, a constable named Fred Lincoln noticed a brand new touring car parked on a lonely country lane fifteen miles north of Detroit. The car was barely discernible in the darkness. Forty minutes earlier Lincoln had chased several couples from the area, and at 2:00 A.M. pulled his patrol car up to the strange vehicle. Leaving the lights on in his car, he cautiously approached. Pulling the back door open, the constable pointed his flashlight into the darkness.

Two bullet-riddled bodies leaned against each other on the blood-soaked backseat. Struggling for composure, he raced to his nearby home and called the Sheriff and the County Coroner. Investigators converged on the scene to find the bodies still warm but their faces unrecognizable, mangled by heavy caliber bullets at close range.

Detroit police detectives identified the men from their fingerprints as Abe Axler and Eddie Fletcher. These two were well known Purple lieutenants and hit men, but most importantly they were also Detroit public enemies numbers 1 and 2.

Both men were unarmed and there was no sign of a struggle. Oakland County Sheriff Roy Reynolds surmised that Fletcher was shot by the driver, who turned around to fire. Axler had been killed by a man sitting next to him in the backseat. As a last ghastly joke, or possibly a sign of contempt, the dead men's hands had been joined together by the killers.

When the bodies were first discovered the police wondered why the slayings took place in Oakland County. At one time the gang was reported to have had three cottage hideouts on Cass Lake and another near Walled Lake.

Sheriff Reynolds knew it was Axler's body. Shortly after he had become sheriff, Axler had offered a bribe to "lay off his slot machines." But Reynolds ordered him out of his office and told him his men would pick up every machine they found. Reynolds said "That was the last time I saw him."

Detectives learned that Axler and Fletcher had spent most of the Saturday night before the murder drinking in a Pontiac beer garden. According to witnesses, they had entered the saloon alone and walked out alone. As they walked to Axler's car, they were joined by two other men—this was as far as the murder investigation would ever go.

Axler and Fletcher, lieutenants of the Bernstein brothers, were known as "the Siamese twins" of the Detroit underworld. They were the Purple Gang's top contract men—thugs specializing in murder. In life Abe Axler and Eddie Fletcher had been inseparable friends and partners.

They were a driving force in the evolution of the Purple Gang. Police described them as "schemers and killers" with a lot of "crazy nerve." Both men had grown up in the slums.

Fletcher had been a featherweight boxer in New York with no criminal record prior to his move to Detroit. Never a great professional fighter, when he arrived in 1923 he immediately fell in with the future Purple Gang. One of the rumors about how the Gang got its name began during Fletcher's fights at the Fairview Athletic Club in Detroit.

In the New York custom of donning colored jerseys, Fletcher wore bright purple. It proved to be the color that would one day land him in the backseat of that bloody abandoned car.

Axler's criminal career included hijacking, rumrunning, drug peddling, extortion, and murder. He and Fletcher were prime suspects in the Milaflores Apartment Massacre. Both had been terrorists in the "Cleaners and Dyers War."

They had known for some time that they were going to be killed. A friend of Axler's told police that several weeks before the murders he had been late for a business appointment when his car wouldn't start. He asked Axler for a ride, but Axler hesitated.

"All right," he remarked, "but don't ask me again. I don't like to let you drive with me along the street. It might not be so good for you, anything could happen to me!"

Friends of the Purples reported that both men had been nervous and distraught for some time. Underworld rumor was that Axler had received $30,000 for a "gun job" years earlier. At first he had been afraid to spend the money because he thought that it was too hot but within the last year he'd taken elaborate vacations and spent copiously. Now he owed money.

In the winter of 1933, Axler and Fletcher had tried to go straight. Fletcher reentered professional boxing as a manager. When money wasn't forthcoming, Fletcher and Axler quit the business. After being arrested as public enemies they used the fight racket as a ploy to demonstrate that they had a legitimate means of support.

OnNovember28th,1933,Mrs.AxlerandMrs.Fletcher, guarded by Purples, returned with their husbands' bodies to Brooklyn for funeral services. Prosecutor Harry Toy began to suspect Axler and Fletcher had been killed by their own gang. The two men had tried to "muscle in" on the rackets of other gang members.

"Everything points to their deaths at the hands of members of their own gang," declared Chief of Detectives Fred Frahm. He indicated that if out of town killers had done the job, other Purples would have been in hiding. But this was not the case, they openly walked Detroit streets.

Homicide detectives thought Axler and Fletcher had attempted to take control of the Purple Gang after more able leaders had been removed by infighting or long prison sentences. Although both were known opium smokers, they were far too wary to have been ambushed easily.

Only somebody whom the two men trusted implicitly could have gotten close enough to put them on the spot. Axler had let one of the killers drive his new car.

By December of 1933, police gathered information that Axler and Fletcher had double crossed Harry Fleisher, Harry Millman, and the Bernstein brothers. Main leaders were being assassinated and gangsters were turning into informants; the dismantling of organized crime had clearly begun.

By 1935 the Purple Gang also lost control of their lucrative Detroit race wire service—a significant decline of power—as the result of internal decay. Underworld gossip buzzed that Abe Bernstein and several lieutenants met with local Mafia chiefs.

Although the Italian and Jewish mobs were cordial, Bernstein was told in no uncertain terms that the Italian mob was taking over the Detroit wire service. The Purples could either resolve it peacefully or go to war. The gang was so weakened by internal killings and long prison sentences, that Bernstein conceded the Detroit rackets to the Italian mob peacefully.

In return, the Italians gave Abe enough money to take care of him for the rest of his life, with what was essentially his pension for retirement from organized crime. Abe was taken care of by the Italians, put out like an aging dog. But he was not the only Purple Gang backbone to concede the gang's defeat and seek legitimacy.

Coming Clean

In the thirties, jailed Purple gangsters sought to prove their innocence in the Collingwood massacre. They did this through political mystery man Isiah Leebove, a former New York underworld attorney and a wealthy Michigan oil operator. The public was outraged when the newspapers reported that Leebove had tried to gain access to murderers Ray Bernstein, Irving Milberg, and Harry Keywell for his former law partner, Fred Kaplan.

The relationship with Kaplan was suspicious. The attorney had been retained by Joe Bernstein to get a new trial for the Collingwood trio. Rumors circulated that Leebove was working with Fred Kaplan to seek pardons for the trio from his friend Governor Comstock.

Leebove's connection to the Collingwood case grew when he was appointed to survey the Michigan prison system. He was questioned about his backgroundandhisrequestsforinterviews,beforeaStateinvestigating committee. State Senator Ray Derham told the committee that Leebove, under the guise of his survey of the prison system, had tried to persuade the official in charge of prison industries, Edward Frensdorf, to intercede in the Purple Gang case.

Leebove admitted talking to Kaplan about the convicted men and claimed that Kaplan told him, "these boys are here because of one of the worst frame-ups I've ever heard of. The prosecutor of Wayne County knew they were not guilty, yet participated in their conviction because he saw political advantage accruing to him. . . ."

The prosecutor from their case vehemently denied the accusations, saying the Purples had been defended by eminently capable attorneys and that none of the three gangsters had taken the witness stand in their own defense. Edward Frensdorf, testified before the Senate committee that he had interceded with Warden Corgan on behalf of the three at Marquette Prison at the specific request of Isiah Leebove.

According to Frensdorf, Kaplan claimed it was customary in New York State for attorneys to conduct private interviews with prisoners. Corgan, however, refused to allow Kaplan to interview the prisoners privately. He further stated that Leebove introduced him to Fred Kaplan, and told him that Kaplan was interested in some clients in Marquette Prison, and did not understand why he should not be allowed to interview them in private.

Leebove later contacted Frensdorf and told him that his friend Kaplan was on his way to Marquette to obtain testimony. Leebove planned to come as well, on an inspection trip. He explained that he thought Kaplan might have trouble and specifically asked Frensdorf to speak to the warden about it.

The interview was ultimately refused. Leebove denied all charges.

The real story was that Leebove was a former New York criminal attorney who moved to Michigan to speculate in oil. He had contributed heavily to Comstock's political campaigns and established a personal friendship with the governor. He was appointed him to conduct a survey of the Michigan prison system sans salary or expenses. None of the criminal allegations were proven by the investigating committee, but the Michigan Democratic Party still did not trust Leebove and castigated Comstock for appointing him.

Leebove's connections to the Purple Gang did, in fact exist, through his Mammoth Petroleum and Refining Company. By 1934 it was the largest independent oil outfit east of the Mississippi, and employed Sam Garfield, a grade school friend of the Purples and other future underworld powers.

Garfield worked for Leebove in the oil fields, learned the oil business until 1933, and was then rewarded for his diligence by gaining the deed to one quarter royalty interest in the Mammoth Petroleum Corporation. A suspiciously generous gift.

He incorporated his new property as the Garfield Oil and Gas Corporation and named himself as president. Former Purple Joey Bernstein was its treasurer. The only change in the gangsters' ways was in the business they conducted. Before incorporating, Garfield decided to deed some of the royalties back to Joey Bernstein.

In an interview Bernstein said the Garfield Corp. was a closed firm. No stock would be sold to the public. The only outside shareholder except those named in the incorporation papers was Isadore Bernstein. When asked how he had gotten into the oil business, Joey replied that he had known Garfield for years, but neglected to mention how.

Both Garfield and Joey Bernstein lived in two of the finest homes in Mt. Pleasant, Michigan. The suave and fastidiously dressed Bernstein paraded around Mt. Pleasant wearing a $12,000 blood red star ruby ring.

When questioned about his past, Bernstein denied that he had even been in business with his brothers and avowed, "I'll sue anybody for $5 million who calls me a racketeer. I never have been a racketeer!"

For all of his efforts to extend legitimacy to gangsters, Isiah Leebove earned himself a gangster's death. He was shot down while sitting in the cocktail lounge of the Hotel Doherty in Claire Michigan. His slayer was a former employee named Carl Livingston. Sam Garfield, mysteriously on the scene when reporters looked into Leebove's death, stated that the trouble between Livingston and Leebove had been brewing for several years.

Livingston was an alcoholic, and his drinking problem created a rift between him and Leebove. According to Garfield, Livingston came to believe that Leebove had cheated him out of some oil leases. He swore that someday he would kill Leebove, but friends claimed that he lived in fear of Leebove.

At Livingston's murder trial in November of 1938, the defense requested a court order for the police records of Joey and Ray Bernstein. They tried to show that Livingston had only acted out of fear that Leebove would send his associates, the Purple Gang, after him. Because of this trial the link between Isiah Leebove and Joe Bernstein was positively established, proving Bernstein's connections to Leebove and Sam Garfield.

Carl Livingston was acquitted on a temporary insanity defense, but ten years later would be found dead in a New York hotel room from an overdose of sleeping pills.

After Leebove was murdered, Garfield took over the controlling interest in the Mammoth Producing and Refining Corporation and disclosed that he was the Secretary and Treasurer of Bernstein Oil and Gas Corporation.

For the next 40 years, Sam Garfield prospered in the oil business. He invested some of his wealth in mob gambling enterprises. Garfield was interested in the Havana Rivera Casino owned by the infamous Meyer Lansky.

In 1964 Garfield convinced Lansky to invest some

$250,000 of his rumored underworld fortune in Mich-
igan oil wells. By the mid-sixties, Lansky's properties
were grossing $25,000 to $30,000 a year. Lansky, too,
had managed to retire as a businessman.

Not many Purple Gang associates fared as well as
Sam Garfield and Joey Bernstein. By 1935, having
relinquished control of the Detroit underworld, Henry
Shorr became the next major leader to disappear.

Chapter 11

The Brothers Fleisher

"Shorr blustered his way through the underworld a big hulk of a man, never well liked, sometimes feared not so much for himself as for his so-called connections, a racketeer suspected of many things by police."

—John M. Carlisle,
The Detroit News,
December 1, 1935

"Do you know the eleventh commandment? It is thou shalt not squeal. I have nothing to say."

—Henry Shorr

On a December evening in 1934 former Oakland Sugar House boss and Purple Henry Shorr left home to meet an associate. He was never heard from again. A series of strange incidents followed.

When police were notified that he was missing, they suspected that Shorr had been kidnapped by the underworld. In an anonymous call, someone claiming to be a member of the Shorr family reported Henry missing. Federal agents became involved, but dropped their investigation when it became obvious that Shorr had been taken for a ride.

The Shorr family insisted that they were in contact with him and that he was alive and out of town on a business trip. It appeared as if the Shorr family were trying to cover something up. The day after Shorr's disappearance, a car owned by Harry Fleisher was stopped by police.

Police noticed that the cushions of Fleisher's car were freshly stained with what appeared to be blood, but Fleisher was released, his name had yet to be connected to the Shorr case.

On January 11th, Charlie Leiter was called to headquarters to answer questions regarding his whereabouts the night that Shorr disappeared. Leiter admitted seeing Shorr but claimed he had no idea what happened to him. Police were well aware that Leiter and Shorr had once been close friends and parted ways after a brewery deal fell through.

Progress in the Shorr case continued to be held back by the Shorr family's refusal to cooperate. On January 14th, Harry Fleisher appeared at police headquarters. He told homicide detectives that he was there to assist them because he was concerned about the fate of his good friend, Henry Shorr.

During questioning he calmly explained to police that the blood seen by detectives on his car was from a nosebleed. Fleisher had lent his car to friends and one of the men had slapped his girlfriend in the face. The stains on the upholstery were the result.

By the time Fleisher appeared for questioning his car had been reupholstered. Specifics about the Shorr investigation were not revealed until years later during the Michigan State Police investigation into the murder of State Senator Warren Hooper.

According to a confidential report long buried in the files of the state police, Leiter and Shorr had acquired breweries through the influence of State Republican Party Boss Frank McKay. When these deals collapsed, Shorr severed connections with his former Purple associates and went into business for himself.

Shorr created competition for his old partners. Police believed that the Purple's Harry Fleisher and Sam "Gorilla" Davis were Shorr's executioners and Charlie Leiter had been the man who put Henry Shorr in the right place for them to do it. There really was no honor among these thieves.

During the subsequent Senator Hooper murder, former Police Inspector John Navarre was interviewed about the case by investigators. He believed Shorr was killed over a money deal involving brewery property. The inspector had also received information from underworld sources that Shorr's body was cremated in an industrial incinerator.

In 1938 Mrs. Mary Shorr and her attorneys traveled to Alcatraz Island Federal Penitentiary where Harry Fleisher was serving time for violating I.R.S. laws. Mrs. Shorr wanted him to help her prove to the insurance company that her husband was really dead, since no body was found.

Shorr's wife was looking to collect on the life insurance policy her husband had taken out shortly before his disappearance and was reported to have included a double indemnity clause if it could be proven that Shorr had died a violent death. It was not her lucky day; Fleisher was hardly willing to volunteer information which would convict him of murder!

For Fleisher to have murdered one of his own mentors in organized crime demonstrated just how badly
the Purple Gang had deteriorated, and how fragile was
the ability of these thugs to feel loyalty to anyone but
themselves.

The Fleisher Brothers

It seemed ironic for Harry Fleisher to have murdered
one of his mentors in crime, but to the underworld it
came as no surprise. Born in Russia in 1903 and
brought to the U.S. as an infant, he was the oldest of
three Fleisher brothers. H.F., as Harry Fleisher would
later be known, had grown up with the original Purples
on Hastings Street. Both Harry and his younger brother
Lou were members of the juvenile Purple Gang. They
attended the Old Bishop School and had only rudi-
mentary educations.

Like most of the members of the juvenile gang, the
two oldest Fleishers graduated into the world of organized crime with the advent of Prohibition. Both Harry
and Lou served their apprenticeships as members of
the Oakland Sugar House Gang, Harry as a bodyguard
for Charlie Leiter. Both Fleishers gained reputations as
strong arm men and hijackers. Lou continued to work
sporadically with the father, Louis Sr., who ran a junkyard while H.F. branched out and as an adult had little
to do with Lou. Meanwhile Sam Fleisher began driving
truckloads of liquor for the Purples.

Harry Fleisher became known as a killer. Soft spoken and slightly overweight with a cherubic face, he
looked and acted more like an accountant than a gangster. There is little doubt that his mild manners and
general appearance lulled adversaries into a false sense
of security, because H.F. was extremely strong and

utterly ruthless. Lou Fleisher developed a reputation as a practical joker and an extortionist. During the late twenties he was known to run his car up on the sidewalk when he spotted a friend and chase him down the street laughing loudly while pedestrians ran for their lives. The Fleishers' father was known for his skill at building hidden gun compartments into the side panels of touring cars. This was a sideline business at the family junkyard.

Lou was the first of the Fleisher brothers to serve time in prison. In 1927 at the age of twenty-two, he was convicted of a truck hijacking and sentenced to a ten year term in Federal prison. By the mid-thirties, Harry Fleisher and his younger brother Sammy were gainfully employed as partners with several other Purples in a large, profitable, illegal still. Although national Prohibition ended in 1933, there continued to be a strong black market in illegally brewed alcohol.

In April of 1936, Harry and Sam Fleisher, Joseph Stein, Jack Selbin, and John Gettleson were convicted in Federal court. The charge was conspiring to violate the Internal Revenue Act by manufacturing liquor illegally. Six other men involved in the case were acquitted of the charges. The original indictments were the result of a raid by Federal agents on a warehouse.

Acting on an anonymous tip, agents of the Internal Revenue Service found a complete distillery, whiskey, and alcohol valued at more than $100,000. Trucks and other equipment used by the Fleishers were seized. Harry and Sam Fleisher, Jack Selbin, and Joe Stein were all charged with operating a distillery and not paying Federal taxes. John Gettleson, who was a realtor, had leased the warehouse building for the gang knowing it was to be used for illegal purposes.

On April 15, 1936, Harry and Sam Fleisher, Joe Stein, and Jack Selbin were sentenced to eight years in Federal prison and a $20,000 fine each. During the trial, evidence showed that Sam Fleisher had acted as business agent for the distillery. It was Sam who made the necessary arrangements for bringing in the brewing supplies and shipping out the finished product. Harry and Sam Fleisher, Joe Stein, and Jack Selbin were eventually transferred to Alcatraz Island Penitentiary.

All four were sent to Alcatraz from Leavenworth. They rode in the same car as Alvin Karpis, Public Enemy Number One on the F.B.I. lists, who would later describe Sam Fleisher as a killer. The Fleishers, Selbin, and Stein served four and a half years of their original eight year term. They were released on June 28, 1940, after receiving time off for good behavior.

Louis Fleisher was born in Detroit on September 15, 1905. As a youngster he was a member of the juvenile Purple Gang. He later went to work for Charlie Leiter and Henry Shorr in the Oakland Sugar House where he worked as a sharker, hijacker, and auto mechanic. At six feet and 200 pounds, Lou was effective at his chosen profession. As an adult he often used the alias of "Fleish." He was first arrested at the age of seventeen, the first of many arrests. Charges included concealed weapons, armed robbery, breaking and entering, violation of the State Prohibition law, and murder.

On July 20th, 1926, Lou Fleisher was arrested in Detroit for the murder of William Glanzrock, who was found shot twice through the head. Detectives had received information that Lou Fleisher and Glanzrock were partners in a bootlegging operation. During an argument over the proceeds from a liquor deal, Fleisher, reportedly, pulled a pistol and killed Glanzrock. Lou was arrested and questioned but later released due to lack of evidence. It wasn't until one year later that Fleisher was positively connected to the Glanzrock killing.

Lou Fleisher, Sam Drapkin, and another Purple named Edward Factor were sitting in the car of Jacob "Butch" Kaplan in front of the Oakland Sugar House. Kaplan had walked up to the car and begun talking to Fleisher when another vehicle pulled alongside. Shots were fired. Kaplan died and Fleisher and the others were held as police witnesses. At headquarters, Lou Fleisher admitted to killing Glanzrock a year earlier in self-defense. Police believed the shooting of Kaplan and Fleisher was an attempt by Glanzrock's friends to even the score. Kaplan had just been in the wrong place at the wrong time. Louis Fleisher was charged with manslaughter in the murder of William Glanzrock. Glanzrock's body was later exhumed for a coroner's inquest. Fleisher was arraigned for the Glanzrock murder but released when, again, a coroner's jury could not find enough evidence to link him to the crime.

On July 10th, 1927, at 8:30 P.M., Lou Fleisher and four other Purples hijacked a truck at Flat Rock, Michigan. The vehicle was enroute from Akron, Ohio, hauling approximately $15,000 worth of auto tires and other rubber goods. The driver and his helper told local police and F.B.I. agents that a Studebaker pulled alongside of their truck at a road stop. Five armed men got out and forced the two truckers to get into their car at gunpoint. Two of the bandits drove away with the truck while the three others drove off in the Studebaker with the hostages.

One of the tankers was observant. He noticed that

one side of the trim on a door panel of the Studebaker was torn in a peculiar manner. He also noted the mileage on the vehicle's odometer. He then chewed up a cigar butt he had in his mouth and spit tobacco juice on the rear window of the car so it might be identified by police later. The gangsters drove back to Detroit and continued driving around the city until about 2:30 A.M., when the truck drivers were left in the street. During the time that they were held hostage, the two men were able to get a good look at the bandits who'd held them at gunpoint.

According to the two teamsters, the gangsters conversed in a foreign language (probably Yiddish), in addition to speaking perfect English. The truck drivers even noted that the Studebaker had disk wheels, carried an extra tire on the back, and that all of the tires were Millers.

On July 12th, 1927, the stolen truck and trailer were found. Soon afterwards a Studebaker fitting the description of the one used by the bandits was found in Detroit. It proved to be a 1927 model painted green. Closer inspection revealed a torn door pocket on the right door and tobacco stains on the rear window. A check of State Motor Vehicle records established that Lou Fleisher was the owner of the car, and a warrant was issued for his arrest.

Fleisher was released to U.S. Marshals to appear before the U.S. Commissioner on hijacking charges. He pleaded not guilty and was held in lieu of a $25,000 bond. He denied owning the car or that he was a member of the Oakland Sugar House gang. Fleisher was put into a police lineup and positively identified.

Four hundred tires which had been taken from the truck were found in a rented garage in Detroit. Fleisher continued to refuse to talk to Federal agents. The officers received information that Fleisher's companions the night of the hijacking were Jacob Kaplan and Morris Sandler, both Purple gangsters. Kaplan was killed several weeks later. Sandler was never apprehended. Fleisher later told police that he barely knew the other two men involved but noted New York accents. Louis Fleisher was the only member of the gang of hijackers brought to trial. On February 29th, 1928, he changed his plea to guilty and was sentenced to serve ten years at Leavenworth Penitentiary.

He was released from Federal prison after serving a minimum term on November 21st, 1934. He walked out of Federal prison into a different world. When he got back to Detroit, the Purple Gang was no longer the dominant force. National Prohibition had been repealed. The old time bootleggers and rumrunners had gone into legitimate businesses or gotten into other rackets. Drug peddling, gambling, prostitution, and labor racketeering had become the predominant sources of income for the underworld.

After Harry and Sam Fleisher were indicted for Federal liquor violations in 1935, the three Fleisher brothers moved to Jackson, Michigan, presumably to help their father in his scrap metal business. In the fall of 1935, Lou Fleisher and Sam "Fatty" Bernstein moved to Albion, Michigan, where they opened the Riverside Iron and Metal Company. Their connection to the scrap yard was used as proof they had legitimate employment for the pending Federal trial in the spring of 1936.

Lou Fleisher used the junkyard as a cover for a safecracking operation. He worked with Chester Tutha, leader of a Hamtramck mob known as the "Lizard

Gang." For more than nine months, this gang operated throughout central Michigan committing burglaries and safe thefts which baffled local and State police.
The gang used a supercharged 1935 model Graham
Paige sedan. Lou Fleisher converted the stolen vehicle
into an armored car into which safes could be rolled
and hauled off to be opened later. The interior of the
car was lined with sheet steel and the side windows
were made of bulletproof glass.

The rear window of the armored Graham Paige
sedan was removable. It could be taken out and replaced by a steel plate with gun ports in it. The center
door post of the vehicle and backseat had been carefully removed to allow large safes to be easily pushed
into the car. A small ramp could be pulled out from
under the floor of the car to allow safes to be quickly
wheeled on with a small hand truck. The rear tires of
the car were protected from bullets by steel guards
which extended almost to the ground.

The gang pulled off a burglary or a safe robbery
on the average of several times a week until the night
of May 11th, 1936. On that night the Isabell Seed
Company in Jackson, Michigan, was broken into and
the night clerk at the hotel next door saw the men moving the safe out of the building and into the Graham
Paige sedan. When he walked out to investigate Lou
Fleisher walked up to him and leveled a sawed off
shotgun. Fleisher ordered the man to get off the street.
Battle Creek police eventually chased the Graham
Paige sedan but lost it.

On May 30th, 1936, the Riverside Packing Company
of Jackson had a safe blown and $1500 taken. The
same sedan was seen. On May 31, 1936, a Michigan
resident reported a Graham Paige sedan parked in a

remote location on the Kalamazoo River. It was obvious that someone was trying to hide it. The garage was directly across from Lou Fleisher's junkyard. The car appeared to have several bullet holes in it. Police went to the garage and investigated.

Through a window they could see a partially hidden Graham Paige sedan with bullet holes on the left side. Inside the vehicle was a small hand truck. Officers from the State Police and Jackson police department broke the lock and entered the garage. They found the car had two sets of plates. Several shotguns, rifles, and revolvers were found inside. Flashlights and burglar tools were also found. A raiding party was then organized and sent to Lou Fleisher's home.

A thorough search produced a nickel plated .45 caliber pistol hidden in a drawer. They also found a receipt for the rental of the garage where the car was found. Lou Fleisher and Sam Bernstein, along with their wives, were arrested and brought to Albion for questioning. They were later turned over to the Jackson police as suspects in the Riverside Packing Company robbery. The police showed mug shots of Lou Fleisher, Sam Bernstein, Chester Tutha, John Godlewski, and Robert Deptla. All were recognized as familiar faces around Albion and Jackson. Police found nitroglycerin, dynamite caps, and fifteen feet of wire hidden in the car. The wire was the same type used to blow the safe at the Riverside Packing Company job.

On June 3rd, 1936, Lou Fleisher and Sam Bernstein were questioned about more than fifty burglaries in and around the Jackson area. At this point, police had not decided upon which case to base a prosecution. On June 5th, 1936, Lou Fleisher was positively identified by the night clerk who witnessed the safe removal.

Kane picked Fleisher out of a police lineup as the man who had held a sawed off shotgun on him, but could not identify Sam Bernstein. Sam Bernstein was held as a suspect in a $7000 drug truck hijacking and taken to Detroit.

Lou Fleisher spent several nights in jail before making bond on the charges. Both he and his wife then returned to Detroit. State Police detectives tried to persuade Lou Fleisher to help them find and arrest Chester Tutha, John Godlewski, and Robert Deptla in return for leniency. Fleisher tentatively agreed to the deal, but after several meetings with Tutha and Godlewski he was not successful.

In early September 1936, the case against Fleisher was dismissed by the Jackson County Prosecutor due to lack of evidence. After much coaxing by Corporal Freeman and other members of the State Police, the Jackson County Prosecutor told Freeman to get warrants against Fleisher in Albion for possession of unregistered guns, receiving and aiding in the concealment of a stolen car, and possession of burglary tools. The prosecutor then explained to Freeman that if Fleisher agreed to implicate the other members of his gang, he would give him immunity in the case and try the others for safe blowing. If Fleisher refused to testify against the others, he could then be taken to Calhoun County and tried on the warrant charges against him there.

Lou Fleisher turned himself in before the warrants were put into effect. On September 14, 1936, he arrived in Jackson with his wife. After talking to a local attorney he went to the offices of the Jackson Chief of Police where the Assistant Prosecutor tried to cut a deal. Fleisher only told him, "I have nothing to say. I would rather be in jail than in a coffin." Fleisher was turned over to Calhoun County authorities on the Albion warrants. He was arraigned on the stolen car charge and for possession of burglar tools. The charges were reduced to possession of burglar tools, and he was released on bail. Fleisher returned to Detroit. He was scheduled to appear in Battle Creek Circuit Court but failed to appear and his $5000 bond was forfeited.

With the heat on Lou Fleisher in the heist racket, he turned to other endeavors after moving back to Detroit. He soon became involved in an old familiar sideline, labor racketeering. Fleisher joined forces with a Purple Gang labor racketeer named Jack Ekelman.

In 1933 Ekelman was instrumental in organizing the Jewish Barbers Association in northwest Detroit. He was the business manager for this labor organization but was dissatisfied with his income. At that time there was a legitimate union organization known as the Master Barbers Association. This union actually worked for the good of all its members to provide benefits. Ekelman was greedy. He wanted control of the Association so he began to use his goon squad to try to muscle in on barber shops which belonged to the Master Barbers.

He soon realized that the job was too big for his organization. Ekelman went to see a local Mafia capo known as "Scarface" Joe Bommarito, who often worked with Purple gangsters in racket schemes. Ekelman offered Bommarito a business deal.

He explained that there was a lot of money to be made for the both of them if Bommarito would help Ekelman muscle into the Master Barbers Association, particularly in the downtown Detroit area shops. They agreed that once the takeover was accomplished,

Ekelman would be installed as the head of the union. Both Ekelman and Bommarito would then share equally in a percentage of the members' monthly dues.

On the night of the next meeting of the Master Barbers Association, Jack Ekelman strutted in accompanied by Joe Bommarito and his henchmen, who displayed drawn revolvers and pistols. Bommarito ordered everyone in the place to be silent. Ekelman then told the chairman of the association that he was taking over. He explained that the Master Barbers Association and the Jewish Barbers Association would be combined into one. The union officers promptly handed everything over to Ekelman: all moneys in the treasury, books, records, and meeting minutes. Ekelman then explained that from then on every Detroit barber shop and anyone employed by the owners of these shops must belong and pay dues directly to him and not to the American Federation of Labor.

The old Master Barbers Association was an affiliate of the A.F.L. The officers were ordered to remove their A.F.L. charter from the union offices, and informed that the new association would be an independent union, not associated with the A.F.L.

News of the racketeer takeover quickly reached Frank X. Martell, President of the Detroit Federation of Labor. Martell called an emergency meeting and told the members not to allow themselves to be forced into Ekelman's union. This was easier said than done. Joe Bommarito and his men went to work smashing windows, throwing stench bombs, and bombing the shops of any barbers who did not belong to their union.

This campaign of terrorism lasted for several months. By the time it ended, almost every barber shop in the city was a member of the Master Barbers Association. Ekelman quickly became a powerful labor leader and joined with other labor organizations to create a greater power base. As Ekelman's power grew, he demanded a larger income from the Master Barbers union. By that time Ekelman's end was already $3000 a month, a tidy sum for the Depression era. Once things settled down and Ekelman decided he was secure in his position, he decided that he no longer needed Joe Bommarito as a partner. He stopped paying Bommarito his share.

Bommarito, who was also a union official, had no intentions of bowing out. Ekelman soon received word that his life was in danger and fled Detroit. He went into hiding in New York City where he remained for six months. Ekelman eventually received word from Detroit that Bommarito was having difficulties with the labor organization as well as the Detroit police and assumed it was safe to return to Detroit. He believed that Bommarito had other, bigger problems.

Upon his return in late 1936 Ekelman attempted to reorganize the Barbers union. It was at this point that he became affiliated with Lou Fleisher. Fleisher decided that he and his associates would take over the Kosher Barbers Union, the Kosher Meat Cutters Union, and the Kosher Meat Bosses Union. He also wanted more control over Ekelman's Master Barbers Association.

Lou Fleisher and Jack Ekelman did not get along and often argued furiously over the division of spoils. Shortly after getting the Kosher Meat Cutters Union and Master Barbers Association reorganized, Fleisher jumped his bond in the pending Calhoun County indictments and left for New York. He had been scheduled to appear for trial in Battle Creek on May 3, 1937. Before leaving the city Fleisher borrowed $500 from Joe Bommarito, as he and the Fleisher brothers were old friends. The money was used as a retainer for Fleisher's lawyer to attempt to settle the pending case against him in Calhoun County. Before leaving, Fleisher arranged for Ekelman to send his $50 a week salary as a union organizer to him in New York.

Ekelman wasted little time in attempting to double cross Lou Fleisher once Fleisher was out of sight. Fleisher was also getting money from two other unions through the collections of Jack Ekelman's henchmen. Fleisher soon received word from his partners in Detroit that Ekelman was cheating him. Fleisher immediately returned to Detroit. He met with Ekelman and discussed the money problem. The partnership was dissolved at this meeting. Fleisher essentially gave Ekelman the Master Barbers Association. Fleisher and his men would continue to control the Kosher Meat Cutters and Kosher Bosses Unions, from which Fleisher was getting a considerable amount of money.

Police later estimated he was taking in more than $2400 a month from labor racketeering. One poultry association was reported to be paying Lou Fleisher and his men $2 per week per store. There were over 100 stores in the association. The President of the Jewish Meat Cutters Association, was reported to be the payoff man to the Purples.

At this point Fleisher was working with Sam Millman, Joe Bommarito, and Hymie Cooper. Millman was reported to have inherited a prostitution protection racket from his older brother Harry. These Purples continued collecting from brothels in Ecorse, Mt. Clemens, Hamtramck, and Detroit. The resorts had been paying

Harry Millman and his men various amounts each week for protection. Protection, in this case, from Harry Millman and his men.

While Lou Fleisher went on the lam in 1937, Ekelman ran into Joe Bommarito one night in a local beer garden. Hoping to get back into Bommarito's good graces, Ekelman offered to pay off Lou Fleisher's $500 loan. He told Bommarito that because he and Fleisher were partners he wanted to take care of Fleisher's debt. Bommarito agreed to the offer. Ekelman was to bring $250 to Bommarito's office the next day and the other $250 the following week.

The next morning Ekelman failed to show up at Bommarito's office. Bommarito called Ekelman and demanded to know why he didn't bring the money. Ekelman told him that he had been drunk and did not remember making the offer. Bommarito told Ekelman to "pay up or it'll be your ass." Ekelman was frightened. He called Sam Millman and Hymie Cooper to accompany him to Bommarito's.

Ekelman told off Bommarito while the others stood quietly in his office. Bommarito then calmly told Millman and Cooper to leave, that this business was between him and Ekelman. The two Purples left immediately. Ekelman then calmed down, apologized, and agreed to pay off Bommarito.

Not to be deterred, Ekelman met with one of Fleisher's collectors, a strong arm man named Dave Krause, whose job was to collect from the Butcher Bosses Union and send the payments directly to Lou Fleisher. Ekelman ordered Krause to stop sending money to Fleisher and to turn over the collections to him. Krause refused, saying that the only way that would happen is if he got orders to give the money to Ekelman directly from his boss, Lou Fleisher. Ekelman threatened Krause, telling him, "You carried the money long enough. Now is the time for you to bring the collections to me." When Krause told Fleisher what had happened, Fleisher was furious. He called Sam Millman, who was supposed to take care of things while Fleisher was on the lam. Millman suggested to Fleisher that the way things stood he should come back to Detroit and handle the situation himself. Fleisher went to Detroit and threatened Ekelman, promising to "kick your head off if you don't lay off of Krause." Once again, Ekelman concocted a story. He told Fleisher that he was drunk at the time and did not remember making any promises to Bommarito or to Krause. Fleisher arranged a meeting with Bommarito to find out the truth. It was decided at this meeting that Ekelman had to go. Days later Ekelman disappeared.

Jack Ekelman vanished while supposedly on a business trip to meet with Lou Fleisher. Charles Leiter had driven along with Ekelman that day. When questioned by Detroit police, Leiter claimed that he had fallen asleep in the car because he had been drinking all day. He did not know whether or not Ekelman had actually seen Lou Fleisher. According to Leiter, when he finally woke up they were back in Detroit riding down Gratiot. Ekelman dropped Leiter off and that was the last he had seen of him. Leiter claimed that he had been with Ekelman all day and that they had met with several owners of Detroit slaughterhouses. Leiter and Ekelman had planned to organize the slaughterhouse workers, but only four workers showed up and the idea was a failure. Afterward, the men sat around and drank. Leiter stated that he passed out in the car.

On April 27, 1938, Highland Park police, acting on an anonymous tip, arrested Lou Fleisher, Jack Sherwood, and Fleisher's wife Nellie. When Fleisher stopped his car, his wife burst out of the passenger side door. She ran into a nearby tailor shop and tossed something into a pile of laundry. In the clothes police found a .38 caliber automatic pistol which had a special device for automatic discharge of all of its bullets. The gun was, in effect, a hand-held submachine gun. Officers arrested all three. Police initially charged Lou Fleisher with being a bond jumper in the Albion burglary tool case. The Fleishers' Highland Park apartment was searched. Inside a large trunk police found what was described as the largest underworld arsenal ever seized in the Midwest.

The trunk contained three Luger automatic pistols, two of which were modified into hand-held machine guns which could hold a 32-round clip, a .38 automatic pistol, a .32 revolver, five silencers, 500 rounds of ammunition, a case of tear gas shells and a gas gun, and a pair of brass knuckles.

Both Fleisher and Sherwood were questioned about the disappearance of Jack Ekelman. Police knew that Ekelman and Fleisher were partners. Law enforcement officials had been looking for Fleisher for more than a year. During questioning, Fleisher insisted that the guns found in his apartment belonged to Jack Sherwood and that he knew nothing about them. In the meantime, Nellie Fleisher threatened to burn down the Highland Park Jail if she was locked up. On the morning of April 29th, 1938, she made good on her threat by setting fire to a mattress in her cell.

Police thought that it may have been a ploy to divert

the attention of guards while Fleisher and Sherwood attempted to escape.

Both men's cells were searched. Guards found that bolts on a window guard in Fleisher's cell were loosened, but couldn't figure out how he'd done it.

Fleisher and Sherwood's interrogations were relentless. Sherwood claimed that he had lived in Detroit for ten years, but could not answer the simplest questions about local streets or even where he lived. The three were prosecuted on violations of the Federal firearms law and charged specifically with not registering their machine guns. The maximum penalty at the time was five years in prison and/or a $3000 fine for each weapon in the possession of the defendant.

The search of the Fleishers' apartment was more rewarding. It turned up clues regarding the disappearance of Jack Ekelman. Ekelman's mud splattered car was found at Woodward and Sibley in Detroit the day after he was reported missing. Police found a pair of muddy shoes in Fleisher's apartment. He told detectives that he had picked up the mud walking around his father-in-law's place in the country. According to Fleisher, he hadn't seen Ekelman in months. A notebook was discovered with sixteen addresses in it. Police identified all of the addresses as disorderly houses in Macomb County, Ecorse, and Wyandotte. Next to each entry was a W or an M. Detectives believed these letters represented monthly or weekly payoffs. Police also found newspaper clippings of Ekelman's disappearance, a picture of Ekelman, and a list of the addresses of every barbershop in the city in a suitcase.

Jack Sherwood continued to deny that the guns were his. He had no local police record so his fingerprints were sent out. On the morning of May 1st, 1938, fingerprints and photos of Jack Sherwood were received at Highland Park Police Headquarters. It turned out that Sherwood's real name was Sidney Markman. He was wanted in Brooklyn, New York for the murder of a Brownsville poultry dealer. It was reported that the twenty-one-year-old was a gunman for a mob which controlled New York City's lucrative, four-million dollar a year, extortion racket. The murder was an example to anyone else who refused to pay protection to the ring. The merchant was killed a short distance from the poultry store he had operated for nineteen years, the bullet finishing off his five year long defiance of the mob.

After being identified, Markman confessed to the slaying. "Yeah, I killed him, so what?" Markman told detectives. Later that day New York City detectives arrived to question him. It was discovered during the investigation into Markman's background that Lou Fleisher's brother-in-law, a man named Lou Satren, had brought Markman to Detroit because he was on the lam for the Brooklyn murder. Satren was married to Fleisher's sister Betty. He figured that Lou Fleisher could put Markman to work as a muscle man in the meat cutters protection racket and planned for Markman to take the blame for the arsenal in Fleisher's apartment. This would prevent him from being extradited to New York on the murder charge. Before Markman could be returned to Brooklyn to stand trial, the Federal Court at Detroit had to withdraw its request to prosecute Markman under the Federal firearms law.

On May 2nd, 1938, Lou and Nellie Fleisher and Sid Markman pleaded innocent to the firearm charges before U.S. Commissioner J. Stanley Hurd. The three were held on warrants containing three counts each.

Each count carried a possible ten year sentence. The specific Federal charge was possession and transfer of unregistered submachine guns. Markman was to face the Federal charges before being returned to New York.

Markman was returned to New York after being arraigned in Detroit on the Federal charges. In February of 1939 he was convicted of first degree murder in the Frank slaying. On February 21st, 1939, the New York judge postponed his sentence because of a Federal court order requiring him to appear in Detroit on the firearm charges. In March, Markman was returned to Detroit from the Sing Sing Prison death house to stand trial. During the Federal trial Detective James Byne of the Detroit police Scientific Lab testified. He described two of the weapons confiscated at Fleisher's apartment as "most deadly" because they had been modified to make them fully automatic. This permitted up to thirty cartridges to be discharged with one pull of the trigger.

"Why do you say these particular weapons are the most deadly known to man?" asked John Babcock, the Chief Assistant U.S. Attorney.

"Because they are uncontrollable," replied Payne. "Once you start firing them you can't stop the fire until all of the cartridges in the magazine are discharged. The guns are of relatively light weight. Consequently, the recoil causes the gun to kick up in such a manner that the person operating it cannot place his shots."

The testimony coupled with the backgrounds of the defendants quickly brought a verdict of guilty when the case was given to the jury. On April 7th, 1939, the Fleishers and Markman were found guilty on a combined total of fourteen counts. Lou Fleisher and Sid Markman were sentenced to thirty years each in Federal prison. Nellie Fleisher received a term of ten years in a Federal detention home. Markman was never to serve any of his Federal sentence. On April 10, 1939, he was returned to New York to await the results of an appeal of his death sentence. On January 18, 1940, Markman was executed in the Sing Sing electric chair.

The Federal conviction was essentially the last of Lou Fleisher's presence in the Detroit underworld. Shortly before Fleisher was arrested on the firearms charge, one of the last of the Purple leaders was gunned down in a popular Twelfth Street restaurant.

Chapter *12*

Harry Millman: Last of the Purple Gang Cowboys

"His number is up and it's only a question of time. He has kept himself on the streets with his guns and his fists. He is going to die one of these days and die violently."

—Detective Harold Branton, August 29, 1937

"Millman had stalked through the underworld for seven years with a chip on his shoulder, rye whiskey on his breath and a robust eagerness to be a tough guy."

—John M. Carlisle

It was Millman who was responsible for setting up and murdering Purple lieutenants Abe Axler and Eddie Fletcher in November of 1933, as Axler and Fletcher had double-crossed him, Harry Fleisher and the Bernstein brothers in a business deal. There was little evidence in Harry Millman's childhood that he would someday become one of the most feared gangsters to ever walk the streets of Detroit.

179

As a youngster he attended public schools, but finished high school in a Kentucky military academy. Possibly Millman's mother and father had sensed the rebellion in the boy and thought that the discipline of a military school might do him some good. Millman had a reputation as a champion swimmer.

He graduated from military school in 1928 and returned to Detroit, hanging around pool halls and eventually becoming a habitué of blind pig hangouts of the Purple Gang. According to one acquaintance, "the older hoods let Harry hang around because he was good looking, had a reputation as a ladies man and attracted women." Millman was also good with his fists and liked to drink. He soon developed a reputation as a barroom brawler. By 1929 Millman evolved into a somewhat uncontrollable Purple Gang hijacker and gunman with a reputation for drinking. He was personable and gregarious when sober but dangerous and totally unpredictable when drunk.

The fact that Millman was an alcoholic, coupled with the perpetual chip he carried on his shoulder made him completely ruthless. He pursued his vocation as a gangster with a vengeance. In eight years of activity, he was arrested twenty-eight times for assault, armed robbery, kidnapping, carrying a concealed weapon, extortion, murder, and operating a gambling joint. These were only the crimes for which he was caught!

In his short but colorful career his only convictions were minor traffic offenses and concealed weapons charges. Millman never spent a single night in jail.

As he grew more successful, Millman became the Hollywood version of a real life gangster, sporting $150.00 tailor made suits, custom shirts and ties, and a thick bankroll. His quick, vicious temper, amplified by drinking, once caused him to beat a girlfriend in front of a restaurant full of shocked witnesses. An observer said that "you could have heard a pin drop in the place."

As Harry Millman's reputation grew, so did his violence. He would sometimes target a particular underworld operation solely because it was run by the Mafia, the now dominant underworld power. When shaking down Mafia protected brothels and blind pigs he would walk in, knock customers off their bar stools, and pistol whip anyone foolish enough to fight.

Millman had to answer for his erratic behavior many times in front of Abe Bernstein and other Purple leaders. It was the Bernstein brothers who were most responsible for keeping Millman alive the last few years of his life. He was the one loose cannon in the Purple's and Italian's cordial relations.

On numerous occasions the Mafia bosses met with the Bernstein brothers and demanded that Harry Millman be eliminated. Abe Bernstein would promise to talk to Millman and "straighten him out." But like many notorious gangsters, Millman began believing his own press. He believed he was alive because his enemies were thoroughly terrorized. In reality, Abe Bernstein's promises were all that kept Millman alive and on the street.

He shook down Italian controlled brothels in Michigan towns on a weekly basis. He would walk into a house, beat up the customers and generally disrupt business, sometimes robbing the customers on a daily basis until the business dropped to nothing.

Millman's last mistake was to muscle into rackets controlled by Detroit's Italian Mafia. His move to take over their rackets created a serious rift between him and Joe "Scarface" Bommarito, brother-in-law of Mafia boss Pete Licavoli. When the Detroit Mafia took over the operations of the Purple Gang, it had been a peaceful transition.

At the behest of the defeated Abe Bernstein, individual Purples were forced to work with the Italians. Millman was the only Purple gangster who challenged the Mafia's authority after the Purples lost dominance.

In 1936 Millman strutted into Sam Finazzo's cafe at Eighth and Fort Street in Detroit. The cafe was a hangout for various Italian gangsters. Millman and Bommarito had a confrontation which ended in a fistfight that lasted over an hour, with Millman coming out on top.

Bommarito was known as the overseer of the Italian mob's street operations, including the Local 299 of the Teamsters and Truck Driver's Union whose member Jimmy Hoffa became a labor organizer. The era marked the beginning of a marriage between organized crime and the Teamsters Union which lasted through Hoffa's disappearance. Both former Purples and associates of the Italian mob were firmly entrenched in Local 299.

Their fistfight was the beginning of the grudge between Millman and Joe Bommarito. Rumors circulated that Harry Millman walked up to Bommarito while he was reclined in a barber's chair with a hot towel on his face. Silently, Millman lifted the towel and spat in his face, then walked out of the barber shop.

This final display of contempt ended Harry Millman. Abe Bernstein turned his back on Harry after that. The period of "sit downs" and diplomacy to protect him were over, leaving Millman and his rogue faction of Purples on their own.

In August of 1937, Millman arrived in Detroit from
a short trip out of town. At about 10:00 P.M. he phoned
Harry Fleisher's wife. Harry was in Alcatraz on the tax
evasion conviction.

Millman invited Mrs. Fleisher out for dinner and
dancing at a favorite Purple Gang watering hole known
as the 1040 Club. The two headed out in Millman's
new car, a symbol of his recent success in the handbook and policy rackets. The pair had dinner and
danced for several hours.

He then sent her home in a cab and stayed on, drinking until the bartender and the owner's cousin were
done with their shifts. When they were ready, Millman
handed the keys of his LaSalle coupe to the valet, who
climbed into the car and turned the ignition key.

A tremendous explosion blew out the windows of
nearby buildings and sent the hood of the LaSalle coupe
onto the roof of a five-story building. The valet was
torn to pieces.

The ten sticks of dynamite that had been packed
into the V-shaped cylinders of the engine block were
meant for Harry Millman, but the assailants had not
done their homework. Millman always gave his car
keys to this valet at the 1040 Club. A silent alarm set
off by the shock wave sent three police cruisers to the
F.G. Clayton Company opposite the parking lot.

A Fire Department Rescue truck rushed the barely
alive and mangled valet to Detroit Receiving Hospital,
where he died shortly after being admitted. In his deposition, police asked Harry Millman why he did not investigate after the explosion.

Millman replied, "Well, when the explosion come I
thought it was the building, and someone, I don't
remember quite who . . . said 'It is your car,' and they

said, 'The colored fellow was in it and he is dead.'"

"Didn't you go back and look at the car?" Millman was asked.

"After that kind of a explosion there was no use in going back there," replied Millman.

Willie Holmes's death was the first car bomb Detroit slaying.

Although he openly continued to walk the streets, Millman had been served a death sentence by the Italian mob because of competition in the numbers racket. He did stop hanging around downtown nightclubs after the 1040 Club incident and now could be seen alone in the Boesky's cocktail lounge on all night drinking sprees and heroin binges.

As if he harbored a death wish, Millman continued to taunt the Italian mob. Shortly after his car was bombed, he shot up a Mafia controlled brothel in a drunken rage. Millman's days were numbered.

On the evening of November 24th, 1937, Millman, Hymie Cooper, and Harry Gross stopped at Boesky's cocktail lounge. The restaurant was unusually crowded that Thanksgiving Eve, and Cooper and Gross left for a movie around 9:15. Millman stayed on to drink.

When Cooper and Gross returned after the movie they rejoined Millman at a table, where he'd picked up two ladies. Just before 1:00 A.M., Millman crossed to the bar.

At the same time two men in overcoats and snap brim hats strode into the adjoining restaurant. No one noticed them walk briskly through the crowded restaurant and disappear into the cocktail lounge. The two men opened fire on Millman from a range of two feet.

The roar of the pistols was deafening. Terrified customers ran for the doors and dove under tables. Trays full of dishes flew in all directions as waiters ran for cover.

Ten slugs tore into Millman's body. The force of the barrage threw him back against the bar. He was dead before his bullet-riddled body hit the floor.

The killers then turned their guns on Cooper and Gross, who'd hid under the table when the shooting began. The gunmen were relentless. Both men opened fire on a customer who crossed their path to the door, pushing past his wife as the man collapsed into her arms.

Because the getaway car was registered to a suspect with a New York address, Detroit police suspected that Millman's killers had been imported for the job. Detective Delbert Raymond of the Homicide Squad was sent to New York City to investigate the alleged car owner. Raymond found that the address on the title didn't exist.

Police admitted that they were stymied by the variety of possible motives. Millman's enemies were legion. Detectives were most interested in Millman's ongoing feud with Joe Bommarito.

By December 11th the getaway car was discovered parked in front of 3750 Richton Avenue in Detroit. Police found a 1937 sedan with the license plate reported by witnesses. Two fingerprints were found on the frame of the left front door.

The fix was in. The vehicle was towed to police headquarters and the left front door removed for evidence. Stains were found on the rear seat that proved to be human blood. Police surmised that one of the gunmen had been injured.

Harry Gross languished in the hospital until mid-December but died without naming the killers. The murders of Gross and Millman were never solved.

Millman was the last rebel. By the mid-thirties there was no longer room in the Detroit underworld for wild cards. The Italian mob gradually supplanted the Purple Gang while one by one the members self-destructed.

The intensely violent nature of the groups was conspicuously absent as one eclipsed another, the transition gradual and ironically peaceful. Or perhaps the peace was due to each Purples' inability to look sentimentally upon anything, including the integrity of their own gang.

Although the decision to get rid of Millman was no surprise, it did involve a shocking twist. It had been jointly made between the Purple Gang and the local Mafia. Here were men who were murderous and criminal, yet intolerant of the uncivilized behavior demonstrated by Millman in violating their agreement.

In the last year of his life the stress of living on the edge had finally caught up to him. It was so well known on the street that Millman was going to be hit that he was unwelcome at most Detroit hotels. Nobody wanted Millman's murder to take place in his establishment.

In 1940 more light was shed on the Millman murder when a Brooklyn D.A. investigation uncovered Murder, Inc.

Murder, Inc. was a journalism's pseudonym for the Jewish and Italian mobsters who controlled Brooklyn. The thugs possessed a national reputation as killers and were actually kept on retainer for contracts all over the U.S. Professional hit men would fly in, kill their victim, and be on a plane to New York before local police could connect the crime to its perpetrators.

This group was estimated to have carried out as many as 1,000 execution contracts in ten years. In 1940 a leader of the Brownsville mob known as Abe "Kid Twist" Reles became one of the most important organized crime figures to ever come forward. He poured information forth unchecked, constructing the first accurate blueprint of a national mob organization years before law enforcement agencies would infiltrate them.

Reles claimed that "Pittsburgh Phil" Strauss and "Happy" Maione were sent to Detroit to kill Millman. The local boys had failed to get him with a car bomb, and as a result, the Detroit mob contacted New York for help in eliminating the problem. Strauss and Maione were two of Murder Incorporated's most accomplished "hit men."

The murder was never officially solved, but these two killers probably finished the job. Both Strauss and Maione were eventually convicted of first degree murder in another killing and died in the Sing Sing electric chair.

Despite the fact that by the early forties, the Purple Gang was no longer a force in Detroit, individual Purples continued to operate. In 1940 Harry and Sam Fleisher were released from Alcatraz. The Fleishers, Morris Raider, Myron "Mike" Selik, and remnants of the gang set up headquarters at a Dexter Avenue bar and grill known as O'Larry's. Here, unbelievably, the surviving Purples planned one of the outfit's most infamous murders. It seemed the old timers simply could not resist a good crime.

Chapter *13*

The Murder of Warren Hooper

"With honesty he lived for honesty he was taken."

—Inscription on grave stone,
Michigan State Senator Warren G. Hooper

It was late in the cold, gray afternoon of Thursday, January 11, 1945. Floyd Modjeska was driving south on a lonely and desolate stretch of highway between the State Capital at Lansing and Albion, Michigan. As he rounded a bend in the road he noticed a smoking car pulled onto the shoulder. Modjeska drove up behind the '39 Mercury sedan, and got out to investigate. As he walked around the Mercury, smoke began to billow from the doors.

A man was slumped over in the front seat, and there was a bullet hole in the rear window. Modjeska glanced at his wristwatch. It was 5:30 and night was falling fast. By now a second driver named Kyle Van Auker had stopped.

189

Frightened and unsure of what to do, both men stood in the rapidly falling darkness and stared at the car. A third motorist pulled up and decided to open the now burning vehicle's passenger door. Howard and Van Auker pulled the body out of the front seat and laid it in the snow next to the car. The men then heaped snow on the victim's smoldering pants and into the front seat of the car in an attempt to put out the steadily growing blaze.

Modjeska finally raced to a nearby farmhouse to summon Michigan Police. After firemen and detectives swarmed the scene, the scenario began to emerge. Campaign literature for the election of Warren G. Hooper for State Senate along with clothing, a shaving kit, and other personal belongings were found in the backseat.

The man had evidently turned his head to look at his slayer. One bullet entered behind the left ear and another at the top of the head. Powder burns indicated the murder weapon had been 8-10 inches from the head.

The body was taken to the Hoffman Funeral Home where an autopsy was performed. The badly charred remains were positively identified as those of Senator Hooper. At first it appear as though a fire had been started at the murder scene to destroy evidence. But it was discovered that Hooper had been smoking a cigarette when he was shot, as though the gunfire was an unexpected eruption from someone he'd trusted.

Senator Warren Hooper had been one of the State's chief witnesses in the Grand Jury's ongoing investigation into graft by government officials. He was also the State's star witness against political boss Frank McKay. The Grand Jury had been called when rumors surfaced that Michigan lawmakers were accepting graft from lobbyists.

The appointed special prosecutor Kimber Sigler had political ambitions. He believed that if he could bring down Boss McKay and his henchmen by convicting them of bribing politicians he could build a great political career. It was known that Hooper had essentially been a gopher in the State government who offered his services to McKay in any capacity and Sigler went after him with a vengeance.

In return for doing favors for Frank McKay, Hooper was occasionally mildly compensated. When called before the Grand Jury, he quickly broke down and admitted accepting the boss's bribes.

Hooper was offered immunity in the pending graft case in exchange for his testimony against Frank McKay et al. In 1944 warrants were issued for the arrest of Frank McKay; Floyd Fitzsimmons, a Benton Harbor promoter; and William Green, a former State Representative. The three were charged with bribing legislators to defeat a horse racing bill.

Referred to as the Totalizer Bill, the legislation would have required the Detroit Racing Association to install a totalizer at the Detroit Race Track. This device was intended to minimize the danger of corruption by computing odds instantly. A totalizer would have severely cut underworld racetrack profits, since most tracks were mob controlled.

Political bosses like Frank McKay were determined to see that this legislation was not passed. Special Prosecutor Sigler believed that Frank McKay was responsible for the Hooper murder based on word on the street. He'd supposedly put up $25,000 in an open contract to have Hooper silenced permanently.

Frank McKay had strong connections with the Purple Gang dating back to the early thirties. Former

Purple mob bosses Charles Leiter and Izzy Schwartz worked for McKay in various capacities for twenty years. Schwartz and Leiter had also acted as his bodyguards.

The Hooper murder had all of the earmarks of a professional underworld hit—excellently planned and executed with precision. A maroon car had been observed by local residents laying in wait where Hooper was eventually murdered. The police surmised that the maroon colored vehicle carried the gunmen.

Hooper had been traveling with someone he knew and trusted enough to drive his car. At the point in the road where the gunmen lay in wait, the maroon car swerved in front of Hooper to distract him. The driver slammed on the brakes, pulled a .38 caliber revolver, skidded to a stop, and shot him.

A passing motorist said he'd seen a small man next to Hooper's car shortly after the murder, a claim which corresponded with evidence at the scene. According to the witness, the man was standing on the driver's side and the door was open. The car was actually blocking the road and pulled onto the shoulder to let him pass before tearing off.

Special Prosecutor Sigler told the press that Warren Hooper's death had effectively killed the State's case against Frank McKay and his associates. Hooper's earlier Grand Jury testimony was useless because the defendants could not cross examine the now dead witness. Hooper had been scheduled to testify the following Monday.

Sigler spoke publicly: " . . . Hooper was killed because he was the star State witness, pure and simple." Investigators had no clues as to the identity of the killers, despite a $25,000 reward put up by the legislature.

After hundreds of anonymous tips, the break in the Hooper case came from a twenty-three-year-old prisoner named Alfred Kurner. From jail, he wrote a letter to the judge claiming that he was at O'Larry's Bar on Christmas night in 1944 when Purple associate Sam Abramowitz called him into the men's room and offered $3000 if he wanted to be in on a job.

Kurner had agreed. Later that evening Abramowitz explained some details of the job. They were going to "knock off" a politician who was about to testify before the grand jury.

Several days later, Abramowitz told Kurner they were waiting on a bribe of the witness. Abramowitz handed Kurner a .38 caliber revolver, supposedly from an arsenal hidden at O'Larry's Bar. Kurner was caught the same night using the gun in a robbery for which he was sentenced to twenty-five years in prison.

Kurner was hoping this testimony might buy him a lighter sentence.

Abramowitz made a full confession after a month of intense questioning. He told police that early in December of 1944 he received a telegram from Mike Selik asking him to come to Detroit's famous gangster hangout, and knew an execution was afoot.

The bar was not only controversial for its patrons but for its owner. Larry "O'Larry" Pollack had grown up with the core group of Purples, and was a close friend of the Bernstein brothers, Harry Fleisher, and other bosses. Pollack was a legitimate businessman who liked to fraternize with gangsters. He also had an uncanny knack for being in the wrong place at the wrong time.

O'Larry Pollack had been a key witness to the murder of a Detroit police officer during the hold up of a business office by the Jaworski gang in the summer of 1928. The gang had then actually kidnapped Pollack shortly thereafter, intending to kill him. Harry Fleisher intervened and Pollack was turned loose unharmed.

Back in the days of the Collingwood Massacre, Pollack had been driving by when he was almost hit by the car containing the Purple gunmen fleeing the scene. When questioned Pollack named the gunmen as Ray Bernstein, Harry Keywell, Harry Fleisher, and Irv Milberg. During the trial, he perjured himself on the witness stand by testifying in open court that these were not the men he saw and was cited for contempt.

And so, in true form, it was at Pollack's "O'Larry's Bar" that Abramowitz met with Harry Fleisher, Mike Selik, and young safecracker Henry "Heinie" Luks. The Purples explained to the two ex-cons that a $25,000 fund had been made available for the murder of Warren Hooper. Abramowitz claimed that the Purples offered him $5000 if he participated in the plot.

Three trips were made to Albion, Michigan, in planning the senator's murder. On the first, "Heinie" Luks, with safecracking explosive expertise, planned to wire dynamite to Hooper's car. This fell through when it was learned that the senator kept his car in a garage.

On their second trip, Abramowitz and Sammy Fleisher drove to Albion to kill Hooper in his office. It was aborted when the killers saw Hooper's wife and children in his office too. On their third trip, the thugs planned to waylay Hooper along the highway between Lansing and Albion.

This also failed when, like keystone cops, they missed the senator's car. By the third failure, the frustrated Abramowitz met with Harry Fleisher at O'Larry's and told him that he was dropping out. Abramowitz told police that Fleisher's response was, "I guess Mike and I will do it ourselves."

"Heinie" Luks was arrested based on Abramowitz's confession and tried to call Abramowitz a liar. When confronted by Abramowitz, he corroborated the story and both were granted immunity in return for being State witnesses.

The warrant specifically charged Harry Fleisher, Sam Fleisher, Mike Selik, and Pete Mahoney with conspiracy to murder Senator Hooper. The unfortunate Mahoney, a Detroit gambler and friend of Harry Fleisher, had nothing to do with the planning of the job and was merely present while the murder was discussed.

During the time that the Hooper murder trial was being held in July 1945, a shocking report made public by the Attorney General revealed the findings of an investigation into the Michigan prison system. It concluded that Senator Warren Hooper's murderers may have been Jackson Prison inmates who had been let out of prison specifically to assassinate Hooper.

Attorney General Dethmers believed that arrangements to murder Hooper could have been made when Mike Selik and Harry Fleisher visited Jackson Prison several days prior to the murder. Defense attorneys filed for a mistrial stating that Dethmers' hypothesis had prejudiced the jury. The motion was denied.

But rumors persisted that if a prisoner was in with the right clique, he could own the men who jailed him. While Mike Selik served in Jackson Prison, he had been Deputy Warden D.C. Petit's houseboy, and would actually drive to Detroit in Petit's car. Petit would get happily drunk at his favorite bar and be entertained by prostitutes at Selik's expense while the latter drove off for the rest of the evening.

The glamour associated with gangsters in the thirties made them seem like exciting mavericks with big bankrolls, even when they were in prison. Ray Bernstein and the Keywell brothers basically ran Jackson Prison in the early forties. These inmates and their friends got any types of jobs they wanted and could essentially leave the prison whenever they liked.

If you were connected with the inner circle of Purple gangster inmates, you would be taken out of prison during the summer months to attend picnics or parties. Ray Bernstein personally ran one of the biggest horse betting books there. According to one inmate, "the whole joint was run on who you were and what you had!" Both Jackson Prison Warden Harry Jackson and Deputy Warden D.C. Petit were in on the action.

Purple Gang inmates often drank at the basement bar of Deputy Warden D.C. Petit's home in the company of various prison officials with liquor supplied by O'Larry's Bar. Reports indicated that members of the Purple Gang, including Mike Selik and Harry Fleisher, were permitted to visit Ray Bernstein and other Jackson inmates privately in Petit's office. The meetings took place approximately a month after the Hooper murder.

Purples, Feisher and Selik, along with several others, were eventually convicted of conspiracy to murder in the Hooper case. Both Selik and Fleisher jumped bonds of $25,000 each and fled the state. Both men disappeared and remained fugitives for several years until F.B.I. agents acting on an anonymous tip surrounded Harry Fleisher and a female companion on a Pompano, Florida beach. For most of the time that Harry Fleisher was a fugitive, he was reported to have claimed to be a traveling salesman.

Close friends said he actually prospered selling cookware.

When asked by Judge Levin if he had anything to say, Fleisher commented, "I was forced to do what I did, I've been given a bad deal from every place." Fleisher now faced a possible fifty years in Federal and State prison sentences.

On February 2nd, 1951, New York police department detectives arrested a man named Max Green as a burglary suspect. Police checked Green's fingerprints with F.B.I. records, and found that they matched those of Purple gangster Mike Selik. Selik admitted his identity, but the only reference he made to the Hooper murder was that he had been persecuted for political reasons and framed in the Hooper case.

Selik was returned to Michigan where he received an additional five years as a fugitive, and, like Fleisher, faced more than fifty years in Federal and State prison sentences. No one was ever indicted for the murder of Senator Warren Hooper. In late 1946, a former Michigan inmate came forward with a fantastic story that made all the pieces of the puzzle fit.

Louis Brown was a recently released parolee. During routine visits to his parole officer, Brown implied that he was holding important information about the Hooper murder. After some coaxing by police detectives and a promise of police protection for the rest of his life, Brown agreed to divulge his secret.

In January of 1945, about a month before the Hooper murder, some Jackson prison inmates, including Ray Bernstein and Harry Keywell, were called to Deputy Warden D.C. Petit's office. At the meeting they were offered $15,000 to kill Hooper by one of Frank McKay's errand boys.

McKay and the warden made a brief appearance to show that the offer was being made in good faith and the group was paid $10,000 in cash with a promise of the additional $5000 when the job was done. They were provided guns, street clothes, and even phony license plates.

The men left the prison in Petit's maroon colored convertible, followed by Warden Harry Jackson. According to Brown, the two men were nervous and jittery when they returned. Brown's story was based on his claim that Harry Keywell had bragged of Hooper's smoothly executed murder to a group of inmates. He'd described how they waited for Hooper to drive past and then forced the senator's car to the shoulder so Ray Bernstein could run up and blast the startled politician.

By 1947 Louis Brown was reciting his story for a group of officials that included the State Attorney General as well as the new governor and former Special Prosecutor, Kim Sigler. He admitted that he had been paid by the Deputy Warden to keep the story to himself. Amazingly, no indictments were handed down from the testimony of Louis Brown, and the Hooper murder remains officially unsolved to this day.

Although the Purples were once powerful enough to execute contracts while in prison, the absence of indictments showed how incidental they'd become to the criminal world. By the early fifties many Purple leaders were dead, and survivors serving life sentences or lengthy terms. The capture and convictions of Harry Fleisher and Mike Selik ended the careers of the last acting Purples in the Detroit underworld.

Chapter *14*

The Prison Years

"Spider Murphy played the tenor sax-o-phone. Little Joe was blowin' on the slide trombone. The drummer boy from Illinois went crash, boom, bang. The whole rhythm section was the Purple Gang."

—Verse from "Jailhouse Rock,"
by J. Leiber and M. Stoller

"I needed correction and I got it. I met a lot of nice people, reputable ones. I learned that crime certainly does not pay."

—Ray Bernstein, 1963

By 1935 the heyday of the Purple Gang was over. At least eighteen members met violent deaths at the hands of one another. The loosely knit organization, predictably, had self-destructed. Abe Bernstein distanced himself from the few active associates of Detroit's underworld to concentrate on what would become a lifelong struggle to get his brother Ray out

199

of prison. Joe Bernstein became a legitimate businessman and moved his operation to California. Isadore
Bernstein soon followed.

Charlie Leiter had been operating a bar in Detroit
since the early forties. When questioned by a *Detroit
News* reporter, Leiter replied, "I work fifteen to eighteen hours a day in this joint, I never go anywhere else,
I never see anybody. I'm content to be a beer glass
guy, a schmuck, selling beer by the glass."

Harry and Sam Fleisher, Jack Selbin, and Jack
Stein had all been convicted of conspiracy to violate
I.R.S. laws in 1936. Paroled in 1940, the Fleishers
returned to crime and by 1945 were convicted of conspiracy to murder Senator Warren Hooper. Convicted
of armed robbery as well, they were poised for life
sentences.

In 1945 a Michigan Attorney General's investigation
revealed that inmates were literally running the state
prison. Among the leaders of the inmate syndicate were
Phil and Harry Keywell, and Ray Bernstein. Also loom-
ing were the allegations of Bernstein and Harry Keywell's
roles in the Hooper murder. Finally State Corrections
Director Garret Hyns ordered the Keywell brothers and
Ray Bernstein returned to the maximum security of
Marquette Prison in Michigan's upper peninsula.

As recently as 1961, an attorney retained by the
families of the two Purple gangsters attempted to persuade the governor to commute their sentences—the
only way one convicted of first degree murder in
Michigan could be eligible for parole. This method of
changing sentences would reduce the men's charges
to second degree murder, allowing them to be released
on time served.

Bernstein and Keywell had served thirty years.

Attorney John Babcock and a chaplain at the State Prison of Southern Michigan, traveled to Kansas City to obtain a deposition from Solly Levine. All that time the Detroit bookmaker had been in hiding, still fearing a gangster execution for witnessing the Collingwood Massacre.

In a sworn statement, Levine repudiated his trial testimony. "I wasn't there, I never went there. I never saw those guys that day," Levine told Babcock. The story sounded as ridiculous then as it did in 1931.

For more than a year the Michigan Parole Board left the commutation request pending. Finally the board recommended that the governor not commute the sentences of the two Purple gangsters. In a letter to the governor, the chairperson wrote, "The parole board feels that more years of imprisonment are needed before both men attain commutation status."

In 1963 Ray Bernstein suffered a debilitating stroke that paralyzed his left side and caused a serious speech impediment. Lawyers now pressed for a mercy parole for the wheelchair-bound fifty-eight-year-old Purple.

Bernstein was wheeled into his final parole board hearing. His spotless prison record of thirty-two years and his contributions to other inmates—including teaching school and contributing money—were taken into consideration. Bernstein told the board that if he was well enough when he got out of prison he wanted to work with delinquent boys.

In 1964 he was released on a mercy parole and admitted to University of Michigan Hospital. In and out of hospitals and nursing homes, Raymond Bernstein died at the U of M Medical Center on July 9, 1966. He was sixty-one years old.

Harry Keywell remained in prison for two more

years, until Governor Romney signed a commutation order. A week later Keywell walked out of the gates of Jackson Prison a free man. He was fifty-four years old.

On October 18th, 1965, Harry Fleisher became the last Purple gangster to be released from State prison. In the late fifties, he'd worked as the chief clerk of the Prison Food Department and organized other convicts for "Operation Leaky Arm," the nickname for annual prison blood drives. Fleisher personally donated thirty-nine pints of blood, making him the top donor in Jackson Prison, an ironic claim to fame, in view of how much blood he'd shed. Something of a jailhouse lawyer in prison, he was preparing his own appeals to seek an early parole.

In 1957, Lou Fleisher was released after nineteen years in Alcatraz. Prison officials called him a model prisoner. When asked by reporters what he thought about juvenile delinquency, Lou replied, "Juvenile delinquency. It's no good. Look at me. I paid with half of my life!" Upon release Fleisher claimed to be going into the scrap business.

A year after release Fleisher and an accomplice named Joey Anielak were arrested at the Dorsey Cleaners branch on Seven Mile Road in Detroit. He'd been suspected by the police due to a sudden rash of arsons in the cleaning industry. Police surrounded the Dorsey Cleaners and watched while Lou Fleisher drilled holes in the roof through which Anielak poured a can of gasoline.

Fleisher and Anielak pleaded guilty to attempting to burn a building. On April 3, 1964, Louis Fleisher was found dead in his cell. The official cause of death was heart attack, Fleisher was fifty-six years old.

By 1950 Philip Keywell had become a prison

trustee. By then the former Purple had served twenty years of the life sentence he'd earned with his 1930 murder. Psychologists called him "hostile with a big shot complex," and his promotion sparked a controversy.

Rumors of payoffs circulated and he was transferred to the Maybury Sanitarium in Northville, Michigan where he acted as the trustee foreman of that institution's chicken ranch. For several years Keywell lived in this minimum security environment until media attention prompted the newly appointed Corrections Commission to take action. Phil Keywell was returned to Jackson Prison.

In 1962 his attorneys attempted to win a commutation of the first degree murder sentence. But for Phil Keywell commutation was an emotionally charged issue. He'd shot a sixteen-year-old boy to death simply for looking into the window of a cutting plant—a truly senseless killing.

The murder victim's seventy-two-year-old mother appeared and pleaded with the parole board to keep Keywell in prison. Philip Keywell's father also made an impassioned and tearful plea.

"Please give me my son back. . . . I'll set him up. I know he'll make up for the past."

Philip Keywell then made a statement to the parole board. "I've regretted the incident all my life. I was twenty-one, naive, ignorant and no doubt a little bit stupid." When asked by a board member if he carried a gun at the time of the Mixon murder, Keywell replied, "I always carried a gun. During the Prohibition era . . . it was the accepted thing—just like wearing an overcoat. Everybody carried a gun."

Governor Swainson decided to commute the sentence of Phil Keywell and several other lifer convicts as one of his last acts in office.

Fleisher and Anielak pleaded guilty to attempting to burn a building. On April 3, 1964, Louis Fleisher was found dead in his cell. The official cause of death was heart attack, Fleisher was fifty-six years old.

Both Philip and Harry Keywell married after their release from prison and spent the remainder of their lives in obscurity as quiet, law abiding citizens. Harry Fleisher spent the time working for an old friend as a warehouse manager at Ewald Steel Company in Detroit. He died in May 1978. Sam Fleisher died of a heart attack at his Florida home in 1960.

Abe Bernstein was found dead in his room at the Book Cadillac Hotel in Detroit in March of 1968, the victim of a heart attack at seventy-five. Mike Selik went back to work for underworld gambling operations and at this writing is still living in a Southfield, Michigan nursing home. Selik is possibly the last living Purple gangster.

In retrospect, the Purples ruled the Detroit underworld for a very short time. Greed, lack of organization, and high profile methods insured their short reign. But their ferocity, and the terror they induced in underworld adversaries and citizens alike built a legend that lives on.

They were pioneers of an enduring mythos in our country's history, that of the murderous, the glamourous and the all-powerful: the American mob.

Bibliography

Books

Albini, Joseph L. *The American Mafia: Genesis of a Legend.* New York: Appleton-Century-Crofts, 1971.

Allsop, Kenneth. *The Bootleggers: The Story of Prohibition.* New Rochelle, NY: Arlington House Pub., 1968.

Bennett, Harry, and Paul Marcus. *Ford: We Never Called Him Henry.* New York: Tor Books, published by Tom Dougherty Associates, Inc., 1987.

Bergreen, Laurence. *Capone: The Man and the Era.* New York: Simon and Schuster, 1994.

Chandler, Billy Jaynes. *King of the Mountain: The Life and Death of Giuliano the Bandit.* DeKalb, IL: Northern Illinois University Press, 1988.

Engelman, Larry. *Intemperance: The Lost War Against Liquor.* New York: The Free Press, 1979.

Feverlicht, Robert Strauss. *Justice Crucified: The Story of Sacco and Vanzetti.* New York: McGraw Hill Book Co., 1977.

Fisher, Jim. *The Lindbergh Case.* New Brunswick, NJ: Rutgers University Press, 1987.

Fox, Stephen. *Blood and Power: Organized Crime in Twentieth Century America.* New York: William Morrow & Co., 1989.

Fried, Albert. *The Rise and Fall of the Jewish Gangster in America.* New York: Holt, Rhinehart, and Winston, 1980.

Gervais, G.H. *The Rumrunners: A Prohibition Era Scrapbook.* Scarborough, Ontario: Firefly Books Ltd., 1980.

Giancana, Sam, and Chuck Giancana. *Double Cross: The Explosive Inside Story of the Mobster Who Controlled America.* New York: Warner Books, Inc., 1992.

Helmer, William J. *The Gun That Made the Twenties Roar.* Toronto, Ontario: The MacMillan Co., 1967.

Henderson, Donald Clarke. *In the Reign of Rothstein.* New York: The Vanguard Press, 1929.

Homer, Frederic D. *Guns and Garlic: Myths and Realities of Organized Crime.* West Lafayette, IN: Purdue University Studies, 1974.

Hostetter, Gordon L., and Thomas Quinn Beesley. *It's a Racket.* Chicago: Les Quin Books, Inc., 1929.

Illman, Harry R. *Unholy Toledo.* San Francisco: Polemic Press Publications, 1985.

Kobler, John. *Capone: The Life and World of Al Capone.* New York: G.P. Putnam & Sons, 1971.

Lacey, Robert. *Ford: The Men and the Machine.* Boston: Little, Brown and Co., 1980.

Lacey, Robert. *Meyer Lansky and the Gangster Life.* Boston: Little, Brown and Co., 1991.

Lavine, Emanuel H. *The Third Degree.* New York: Vanguard Press, 1930.

Lutz, William W. *The Detroit News: How a Newspaper and a City Grew Together.* New York: Little Brown, 1973.

Lyle, John H. *The Dry and Lawless Years.* Englewood Cliffs, NJ: Prentice Hall, Inc., 1960.

Lynch, Dennis Tilden. *Criminals and Politicians.* New York: The MacMillan Co., 1932.

Maas, Peter. *The Valachi Papers.* New York: Putnam, 1968.

Messick, Hank, and Burt Goldblatt. *The Mobs and the Mafia: The Illustrated History of Organized Crime.* New York: Thomas V. Crowell Co., 1972.

Messick, Hank. *Lansky.* New York: G.P. Putnam and Sons, 1971.

Messick, Hank. *The Silent Syndicate.* New York: The MacMillan Co., 1967.

Mezzrow, Milton (Mezz), and Bernard Wolfe. *Really the Blues.* New York: Random House, 1946.

Nash, Robert. *Bloodletters and Badmen: A Narrative Encyclopedia of America Criminals from the Pilgrims to the Present.* New York: H. Evans & Co., 1983.

Nash, Jay Robert. *World Encyclopedia of Organized Crime.* New York: Praeger House, 1992.

Neff, James. *Mobbed Up: Jackie Presser's High Wire Life in the Teamsters, the Mafia and the F.B.I.* New York: Atlantic Monthly Press, 1989.

Nelli, Humbert S. *The Business of Crime: Italians and Syndicate Crime in the United States.* New York: Oxford University Press, 1976.

Nickel, Steven. *Torso: The Story of Eliot Ness and the Search for a Psychopathic Killer.* Winston-Salem, NC: John F. Blair, Publisher, 1989.

Nown, Graham. *The English Godfather: Owney Madden.* London: Ward Lock Limited, 1987.

Pasley, Fred. *Al Capone: Biography of a Self Made Man.* New York: Garden City Publishing, 1930.

Pasley, Fred D. *Muscling In.* New York: Ives Washburn Pub., 1931.

Peterson, Virgil. *The Mob: Two Hundred Years of Organized Crime in New York.* Ottawa, IL: Green Hill Pub., 1983.

Reid, Ed. *The Grim Reapers: The Anatomy of Organized Crime in America.* Chicago: Henry Regnery Co., 1969.

Rockaway, Robert A. *But He Was Good to His Mother: The Lives and Crimes of Jewish Gangsters.* New York, Jerusalem: Gefen Books, 1993.

Roemer, William F., Jr. *Accardo: The Genuine Godfather.* New York: Donald F. Fine Publishers, 1995.

Roemer, William F., Jr. *The Enforcer: Spilottro: The Chicago*

Mobs Man Over Las Vegas. New York: Donald I. Fine, Inc., 1994.

Rubenstein, Bruce A., and Lawrence E. Ziewac. *Three Bullets Sealed His Lips.* E. Lansing, MI: Michigan State University Press, 1987.

Rudensky, Morris (Red). *The Gonif.* San Francisco, CA, Blue Earth, MN: The Piper Co., 1970.

Schoenberg, Robert J. *Mr. Capone.* New York: William Morrow and Co., 1992.

Seidman, Harold. *The Labor Czars: A History of Labor Racketeering.* New York: Livernight Pub. Co., 1938.

Smith, Dwight C., Jr. *The Mafia Mystique.* New York: Basic Books, 1975.

Sojourn, Frederic. *The Brotherhood of Evil: The Mafia.* New York: Farrar, Straus and Kudahy, 1959.

Sullivan, Edward D. *Rattling the Cup on Chicago Crime.* New York: The Vanguard Press, 1929.

Sullivan, Edward Dean. *Chicago Surrenders.* New York: The Vanguard Press, 1930.

Sullivan, Edward Dean. *The Snatch Racket.* New York: The Vanguard Press, 1932.

Turkus, Burton B., and Sid Fedor. *Murder Inc.: The Story of the Syndicate.* New York: Farrar, Straus and Young, 1951.

Willemse, Cornelius W. *Behind the Green Lights.* New York: Alfred A. Knopf Co., 1931.

Woodford, Arthur M., and Frank B. Woodford. *All Our Yesterdays.* Detroit: Wayne State University Press, 1969.

Court Cases

People of the City of Detroit vs. Buckie Baumann et al., Detroit Recorders Court Case No. 72183.

People of the City of Detroit vs. Charles Jacoby, Abe Bernstein et al., Detroit Recorders Court Case No. 80627.

People of the City of Detroit vs. Philip Keywell, Detroit Recorders Court Case No. 97257.

People of the City of Detroit vs. Morris Raider et al., Detroit Recorders Court Case No. 75026.

People of the City of Detroit vs. Harry Fleisher, Detroit Recorders Court Case No. 4196.

People of the City of Detroit vs. Harry Millman et al., Detroit Recorders Court Case No. 98661.

People of the City of Detroit vs. Sam Rosenberg alias "Hunky Sam," Detroit Recorders Court Case No. A2487.

The People vs. Raider, The Supreme Court of Michigan, December 8, 1931, Case No. 212, in Northwestern Reporter, 387.

Court Records

F.B.I. File No. 48-924
F.B.I. File No. 58-15731
F.B.I. File No. 15-108-28

Magazines

Belknap, Tim. "The Purples Remembered." *Detroit Free Press Magazine*, Sunday, June 26, 1983.

Berger, Meyer. "Murder Inc. Justice Overtakes the Largest and Most Cruel Gang of Killers in U.S. History." *Life Magazine*, Sept. 30, 1940.

Kelman, Maurice. "Ray Girardin's Detroit." *Detroit Free Press Magazine*, Sunday, May 14, 1972; Sunday, May 21, 1972.

Maas, Peter. "Mafia: The Inside Story." *Saturday Evening Post*, August 17, 1963.

Rockaway, Robert. "Detroit's Purple Gang: Not So Nice Jewish Boys." *The Jewish News*, June 19, 1990.

Newspapers

Bay City Times
Detroit Evening Times

Detroit Free Press
Detroit News
New York Times

Reports

Widner, Edward J. *History of the Notorious Detroit Purple Gang*. Special Report: Detroit Police Department Criminal Information Bureau, May 10, 1963.

Miscellaneous

Leiber and Stoller. 1958. "Jailhouse Rock."

Index